To Armenians with Love

The Memoirs of a Patriot

HOVHANNES MUGRDITCHIAN

To Armenians with Love

The Memoirs of a Patriot

Paul Mart
7637 S.E. Teton Drive
Hobe Sound, Florida 33455

Edited by Christopher Gilson and Paul Martin.

Contents

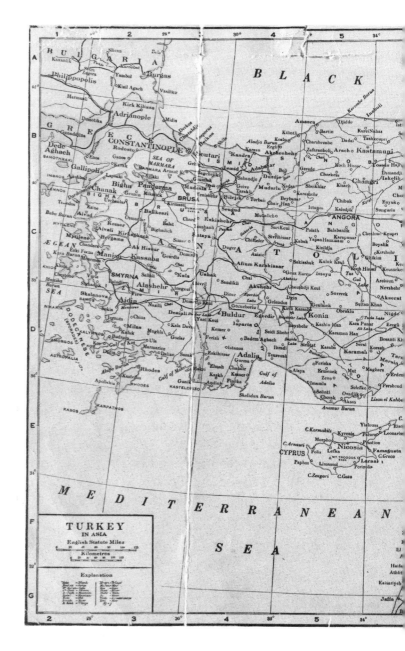

Turkey–Circa 1921

viii

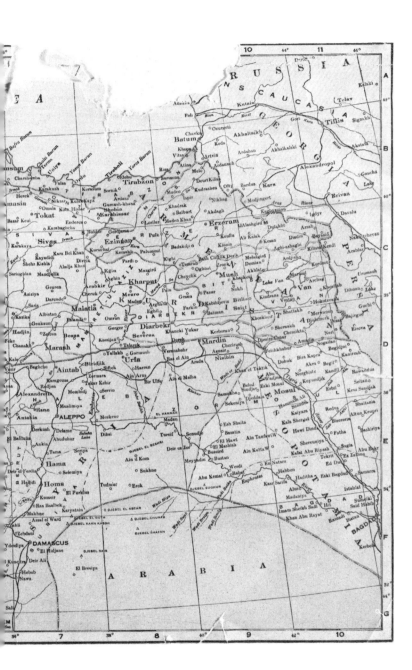

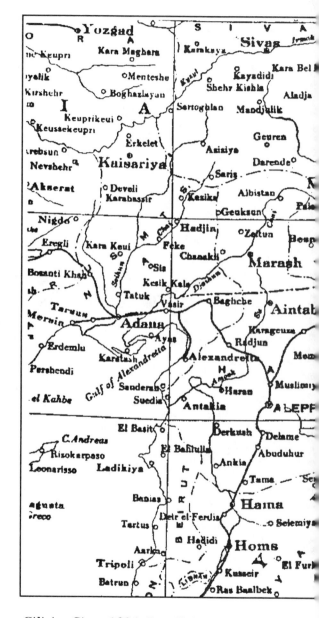

Cilicia–Circa 1921–Detailed Area

Gerdjama
Ezingan
Pulk
Keull
Kemakh
Palumout
Badakdji
Klunis
Pardi
Kighi
Temran
Bash Chiftlik
Egin
Mazgird
Oghnut
Agbin
Kharput
Cheyelik
Mus
Palu
Mezre
Pasur
Gesan
Maden
Arghana
Kabildjevis
Farkin
Eghil
Omrun
River
DIARBEKR
Batman
Diarbekr
Gerger
Severek
Khaneki Yukar
Kerboran
Knodjan
Derek
Mardin
Talarek
Cherie
Yallakh
Garmush
Veranshehr
Asnair
Urfa
Ras el Ain
Nisibin
Arada
Siftek
Harran
Ain Arus
Ain el Melha
Kebir
Bir Ulfe
Serrin
Khabur
Nahr Belikh
Meskene
EL HAMMAR
Madan
Esh Sh
Dibsi
Tureif
Seendje
El Hawi
DJEBEL EL BESHRI
Deir es Zor
El Mashish
Buseird
Ain il Kom
Meyyadin
Bustan
Sukhne
Abu Kemal
Erek
DJEBEL SUGHUR
Wadi Ratka
Wadi Miya

Present-Day Turkey

Detailed Map of What Formerly was Cilicia

Arapkir Tuncell Bingöl

eklmhan Vertek Murat

Keban Barajı Keban Murat Genç

Darende Elâzığ Harput Palu

Hasar Gölü Hani Lice

Akçadağ Maden Silvan

Malatya K Ergani U

Elbistan Pütürge Batman

anlı Doğanşehir Çermik Beşi

Gölbaşı Adıyaman Diyarbakır Bismil

Besni Fırat (Euphrates) Siverek Dicle Tigri

aş Samsat

Kızılin Karakeçi

Halfet Firat (Euphrates) Derik

Nizip Urfa (Edessa) Mar

Birecik Viranşehir

Jarābulus Ceylanpınar Al Qāmishli

Harran Ra's al 'Ayn

691 Akçakale

Manbij Tell al Abyad Tell Halaf ta

Al Bāb Abū Daghmah Al Ḥasakah

alab (Aleppo) 631 Khābūr

Fath Thawrah Buhayrat al Asad

dikh (Ebla) Al Furat Ar Raqqah

ar Nu'man Aş Sabkhah M

kia) (Euphrates) Zenobia

lamath) Tibni Aş Şuwar

867 Bishri Dayraz Zaw

xv

Preface

These memoirs left by my father, Hovhannes Mugrditchian, are in a very real sense a love story. Not a story of one individual's love for another, but of a patriot's lifetime devotion to his people.

From his boyhood days in Cilicia at the turn of the century until his death in April 1974, my father worked for the well-being of his fellow Armenians.

Along with a resolute will to survive, his devotion carried him and his young wife, Beatrice, through the desperation and horrors of the Armenian genocide during World War I. It did not diminish when renewed terrorization of Cilicia forced my parents' escape to America. His devotion compelled him and his wife to repatriate to Soviet Armenia after World War II so that he could help rebuild his homeland.

A remarkable memory served him well late in his life. He spent long hours writing in his native tongue about his personal experiences and about events that shaped not only his own destiny but that of the Armenian people.

A bound copy of the volume he wrote is shared with my

two sisters as a treasured family possession. In the late 1980s, our uncle, Gaspar Arakelian, who had settled in Mexico and had become a successful businessman there, felt it would be wise to have the contents transcribed on tapes also. This was done by his friend, H. J. (Jack) Sevakian, who resides in Canada. For our children and grandchildren, we knew we had to have an English-language version. I am grateful to Dr. Arra S. Avakian, a family friend and retired professor of Armenian studies, at California State University in Fresno for this translation.

My father's life personified the indomitable spirit and resolve that had brought the Armenian people triumphant through centuries of persecution and attempted annihilation. A writer friend, Christopher Gilson, volunteered to work with me on the material and form it into a narrative journal. My sisters, Anna and Martha, and I are thankful to Mr. Gilson for his expertise and the great amount of time spent. This is a story our descendants will treasure and others will enjoy.

Paul (Mugrditchian) Martin

– I –

Escape to Safety

In starting these memoirs, it is important to revisit fateful events of the late eighteenth century. For they determined where my forefathers, the Mugrditchians, settled and where I was born.

Because so few persons could write in those earlier times, the custom was to hand down history orally from one generation to the next. In our case, the primary source was my grandmother. She was called Cherub Lamb and lived to be more than 112 years of age. She told our story to her son Asadour, my father's brother, and to my brother Khacher, who in turn relayed it to me.

Cilicia, the Armenians' largest single homeland until after World War I, serves as a backdrop for this story and for my chronicle of survival in the present century.

– A Matter of Honor –

About 1780, the beautiful young daughter of an esteemed Armenian family of Marash (now Maras) was raped by a high-ranking Turkish official. Cilicia and other Armenian enclaves in the vast Turkish empire were under the jurisdiction of regional Turkish chiefs assigned by a loosely structured, sultan-directed central authority in Constantinople. Armenian settlements were permitted to have their own local officials, however, with the church often the major force.

When news of the young girl's painful and humiliating experience reached community leaders in Zeitun (now Suleymanli), an active center upriver from Marash, they convened a committee to consider the matter. To defend Armenian honor, they decided to seek vengeance against the guilty Turk. One of the leaders, Huge Sarkis, inspired by deeds of famed Saint Sergius (Captain Sarkis), proposed that he be the avenger. All present readily agreed that he was the logical man to carry out the dangerous mission.

Sarkis proceeded immediately. Wearing clothes of a beggar, he went to Marash. Hidden in the clothes was the "Blessed Dagger" of Zeitun, a weapon enshrined in the lore of past Armenian heroism.

Marash is bounded on the north by the Akher Mountains. To the south are foothills and open fields. At the higher elevations beyond the city are many cool springs surrounded by willows. On hot summer days, especially Fridays, Turkish officials liked to go there to relax. They would stay up until late at night, drinking, eating, and enjoying themselves at the expense of the Armenian inhabitants.

When Sarkis arrived, he set out cautiously to determine which official had raped the Armenian girl. By posing as a beggar and listening to everything he heard around him, he succeeded in learning the man's identity.

Late on a Friday night, Sarkis moved close to a group

of reveling Turks. They were drunk. Carefully, he approached one of them.

"A piece of bread for a beggar," he pleaded.

As the official reached over to hand him a morsel of bread, Sarkis moved with lightning speed. The Blessed Dagger of Zeitun pierced the man's heart. Sarkis flew off like an eagle, quickly disappearing in the mountains. In their drunken stupor, totally dumbfounded, the Turks were unable to pursue him.

In two days, Sarkis was back in Zeitun. He told the leaders what had happened. Overjoyed, they praised him for his bravery.

Meanwhile, in great anger, the Turkish government was looking for the killer. But no one in Marash had any idea of who he might be. Because of the incident and the government's frustration in not being able to solve the mystery, Armenians in Constantinople began to be subjected to severe persecution.

Aware of the intense wrath of the Turkish sultan in Constantinople, the leaders of Zeitun again held a meeting. For his own sake and the people's security, they recommended that Sarkis leave and take refuge in the Amanus Mountains under the protection of chieftains Hassan Bey and Alageoz Oghlou.

It is believed these two valley chieftains were descendants of the Arsacid Dynasty. Although difficult conditions had forced them to embrace Mohammedanism, they remained strong enemies of the Turks. As outlaws, they were in control of the region around the Amanus Mountains, ruling over a large number of villages. Turkish troops had not been able to penetrate those parts.

Sarkis agreed to the plan and traveled to the village of Oerenjik, where chieftain Alageoz lived. Sarkis went to him and told him what had happened. Alageoz was delighted, so much so that he declared: "You will be my bodyguard from this day on. I've been looking a long time for a brave and clever fellow like you." And he assigned Sarkis a room next to his house.

Sometime later, the two of them left Oerenjik and moved about an hour's distance farther up the slopes. There they built a house and called it Gash Obase (the Gash room or dwelling). The location was just south of the later-to-be-established village of Lapajle, my birthplace.

—Tragedy for the Amanus Chieftains—

On orders from the Turkish sultan, the persecution extended to enlistment of very young Armenian boys into the Yenicheris (special crack troops).

The Yenicheris date back to 1328. In that year, Sultan Ourkhan issued an edict to mobilize (devshirme) all Christian boys five to six years old who were subjects of the Ottoman Empire. The children were trained to be fierce fighters who recognized neither race nor parents and were without conscience or pity. A dervish later named them Yenicheris (new soldiers). Ourkhan's objective was to build an army and expand the empire at the expense of the Christians.

To escape the wrathful orders that came in the late eighteenth century, some families in the cities of Chokhak and Kars Bazar, five to six hours east of Sis (now Kozan), left hurriedly to seek security in the Amanus Mountains. They preferred living under the authority of the chieftains to giving up their children. All told, there were six or seven of these families, and they established what later became the village of Lapajle. It is to them that the Mugrditchian lineage can be traced.

Free from Turkish oppression, the families lived under the rule of Alageoz Oghlou. But in 1827, an epidemic of cholera broke out among the residents of the Amanus region. Many died. The news reached Constantinople. The sultan saw in the dire situation an opportunity to wipe out the chieftains and put the residents under his control. He summoned his faithful adviser, Mgrdich Emin, and directed him to accompany a Turkish army to the Amanus region. His orders were that only the chieftains, families and all, were to be wiped out, but that no harm was to come to the other villagers.

Under the leadership of Mgrdich Emin, the army reached Hasan Bey's village with virtually no resistance. After killing that chieftain and his family, the army moved on to Gash Obase, Alageoz Oghlou's home. The Turkish commander tried to capture Alageoz alive, but the proud rebel preferred to kill himself rather than be taken. He threw himself down from the heights of Kara Kaya (Black Rock). His entire family then was liquidated.

Thanks to Mgrdich Emin, the six or seven Armenian families remained free of all danger in Lapajle. They declared their loyalty to the sultan and the region came under the governmental authority of Adana.

Many decades later, my brother Khacher, while grazing goats, came upon the damaged sword that had belonged to Alageoz Oghlou. It was in the forest at the bottom of Black Rock; the Mugrditchian house was on a hill near there. Khacher had the sword repaired and kept it.

My Early Years

I was born into a farming family in the village of Lapajle, which is part of Baghche (now Bahce), April 20, 1888. It was just two weeks after my father's death. I was named Hovhannes for him and baptized in the Saint Asdvadzadzin (Holy Mother of God) church.

Three days before Palm Sunday, my father had gone to the village of Kuzul Aghaj, where he had relatives, to purchase supplies for the household. On Friday, an earthquake occurred. The home in which he was staying began to shake violently. My father, along with others, ran outside. But he remembered that the lady of the house was still inside, lying near the fireplace alongside her newborn infant in a cradle. He rushed back to save them, rousing the mother and gathering up the cradle. Before he reached the doorway, the main ceiling beam of the house crashed down on his head. He died instantly. Although the mother and infant were wounded, both lived.

Thus my father sacrificed his own life to save those of others. His body was brought back to Lapajle, and on Palm Sunday, he was buried beside his ancestors.

This sorrowful accident left his young wife, Martha, hardly twenty-six years of age, a widow, and his four small children fatherless. My mother toiled and suffered greatly to support the four of us. She went through unimaginable difficulties but always succeeded in overcoming them. She denied herself much to provide a livelihood for her children, but found her happiness in us.

I remember as a small child how she would go into the forest to gather firewood. One day, as she arrived back with a heavy load on her back, she threw it down at the door of our house. Suddenly a snake slithered out of the bundle of wood. Fortunately, my brother Khacher was able to kill it with an axe.

This was how our life went.

From family members I know that when I was hardly two years old, I became extremely ill. My mother, on her knees at my bed, prayed fervently for me and vowed that if I recovered, she would send me to school.

By the time I was ten years old, I was a spoiled child. My grandmother, my uncle Sunukji Asadour (my father's brother, a chiropractor), and all the other members of the family doted over me because I was the youngest one and bore my father's name.

As to my mother's vow, the balcony of the St. Asdvadzadzin Church had been converted into a school, and she enrolled me. I remember the slate board they hung from my neck. It had the letters of the Armenian alphabet.

Right next to the church was a large walnut tree with a small stream running by it. We played there at midday, often getting one another wet. One day a boy two years older than I threw a large rock into the water and got me well soaked. To get even, I picked up a rock and instead of throwing it into the water, aimed at him. It hit him on the head. I ran from the school so I wouldn't be punished. No matter how much I was pressed, I wouldn't go back to school. The teacher came to our house several times, promising that I would not be punished if I returned. But I still refused go to. That, I'm glad to say, was not the end of my schooling, however.

In 1898, through a gift from a wealthy Russian Armenian, Krikor Shatsian, an orphanage school was opened in the Sis monastery. (The word orphan frequently is interpreted to mean a child who has lost both parents. But it also applies to one-parent children, and this was the case with Armenian orphanages.)

The school was opened mainly for children left behind in the Turkish massacres of 1895–1896. Perpetrated by Sultan Abdul Hamid II to "curb the zeal" of Armenians for independence, those bloodthirsty killings annihilated some three hundred thousand people. And, alas, they were not the last of Turkish attempts to destroy us!

For the school, orphans were sought from villages of Cilicia. My mother appealed to the vicar of Baghche, an influential leader who was from Zeitun, to get me selected from our village.

In those days, people could not travel long distances from their homes unless they were registered in the government census. Families of young males who were registered had to pay military conscription escape fees. In order to avoid their having to do so, our mayor had not registered boys of many of our poor families. I was among them. But one boy, Vartevar Demirjian, was registered. His family agreed to have me sent under his name to the newly opened school. I was the first boy to leave our village for an education.

—In School to Stay—

As Vartevar Demirjian, I was enrolled in the first grade. My age and size were greater than those of my classmates. During classes, I would bend my knees to look smaller. In the course of time in this new environment, I fortunately changed from being a spoiled boy to becoming a top student. One way I did this was to make friends with those who were particularly smart and get them to help me with my lessons.

In the summer we slept on the roof after the night watchman had gone to his cubicle. I would take my book out from under my pillow and read my lesson by moonlight. Through hard study, I was able to skip two grades within two years and join in with boys of my own age and size, something that gave me much satisfaction.

The superintendent of the orphanage, a wonderful man, was Rev. Yeznig Der Sarkisian from Hadjin. He looked after us like an ideal father, and I have always remembered him with great affection.

During the summer recess one year we were taken for two months to the far-off Yuzbey summer place of the revered Roubinyants princes. What a memorable experience it was!

Often we would climb the slopes of the Yuzbey Mountains, competing with one another to reach each of the three summits. From them we could see the entire fortified city of Vahgo and the mountains of Hadjin. To the west were the Caesarea (Kayseri) regions of the Taurus Mountains and the towering Argeos (Erciyes) peak. And to the east we marveled at the incomparably beautiful scenes spread before us by the Seyhan and Ceyhan rivers.

The glory of this enchanting scenery awakened in us a growing, strengthened feeling of patriotism. We were inspired by recalling the history of old Cilicia. In our hearts we relived the wonderful works of the Roubinyants princes, often singing, "If Only I Could Reach My Goal" ("Nbadagis Hasnim Miayn"). Was it any wonder we returned to the Sis monastery fully invigorated?

Sundays at the monastery were always especially enjoyable. We would climb up to the Levon fortress of Sis, a structure that, in its day, had been impenetrably protected against any enemy horde by the swords of its resolute defenders. It was amazing how well equipped the fortress was, with storage space for provisions that could hold out for long periods. In the center there was even a miraculous spring that provided a continuous flow of cool, clean water. It was said the water came a great distance through subterranean pipes. We never tired of using our imaginations to plan and fight battles in defense of "our fortress."

On some summer nights, to avoid the stifling heat, we would sleep on roofs of structures on the east side of the monastery's courtyard. This was not without its moments of fun!

By order of Sultan Hamid (the "Red Sultan"), the Very Reverend Karekin Khachadourian was confined to house arrest in the monastery. At night he would stroll around the courtyard talking to himself, sometimes cursing the sultan. On hearing this and seeing him, we would break out laughing. He would stop his chatter and look up at us. When we overdid it, he would call out, "I order you to get back in bed and go to sleep." (In rhyme: "Karoz gou dam, mudig urek; angoghnit mech dudig urek.")

Later, Rev. Khachadourian became a bishop and

served as primate in many locations. Eventually he was the exalted patriarch of Constantinople, the spiritual and civil head of all Armenians in Turkey.

A reference should be made to our cook at the orphanage. He was a short-statured, happy and carefree man from Zeitun, and he had a donkey. During the hot days of summer, there always was a shortage of water for kitchen needs. He would go with his donkey to fetch water from the Seyhan River. But that isn't the whole story about the donkey.

The Turkish government buildings and mosque were situated in the fields just below our monastery. Five times each day the hoja would sound out the ezan (Islamic call to prayer). When the Islamic priest (iman) would loudly intone "Allah Ekber" (God is great), the donkey would bray just as loudly. All of us would almost die with laughter. The donkey was so trained that it never failed in its duty to bray.

The orphanage and the seminary were fortunate in having highly qualified teachers. The orphans and the seminarians were taught in the same classroom. The seminarians sat at desks in front, the orphans in the rear.

One of the teachers was Bedros of Palou, later ordained a priest. Another was Rev. Yeghishe Garoian, who became a bishop and vicar of the catholicosate of Cilicia. A third was Haroutiun Kederian Effendi, who had mastered several languages and served not only as translator but as accountant for the monastery. In 1900, Haroutiun Effendi, an extraordinarily patriotic and forward-looking man, was vicar of the catholicate during the reign of Bishop Giragos Bekmejian.

Also at the monastery were several mature seminarians who were to become vartabeds (celibate priests) or kahanas (noncelibate priests). Among them were subdeacons Yeprem Asulian (Dohmouni) and Khat Achabahian. Both later became bishops, Dohmouni as primate of Damascus, Khat as vicar of the catholicate of Cilicia.

In class one day, Yeprem asked Haroutiun Effendi this combination of questions: "What is the present condition of Armenians and what about the future? Can we hope for liberation from the Turkish yoke that so dangerously binds us?"

Haroutiun Effendi's answer became indelibly fixed in my memory: "Armenian political parties were established for the purpose of liberating the Armenians. (Several were organized between 1885 and 1890.) However, because the leaders were inexperienced, the Armenian people were subjected to many trials and tribulations. You know about the massacres of 1894–1896, the occupation of Ottoman Bank in Constantinople, and the sultan's terrorism that resulted in the loss of three hundred thousand Armenian souls, leaving innumerable orphans of whom some are seated right back of you.

"Thus, as I see it, Armenians should not carry out open demonstrations. It is not possible for an unprotected and unarmed people to overthrow an armed government and establish sovereignty. Therefore, we must wisely try to find a powerful government that will stand in support of the Armenians. When the right opportunity arrives, then it becomes possible to think about liberation. There is no other way. The important point is that the people must continue physically to exist."

How sound and pertinent those words were. The political parties that had emerged were rebelling against the oppressive rule of the Red Sultan, Abdul Hamid II. Their common objective was to gain autonomy and independence for Armenians throughout the Ottoman Empire. With the militant ones, the only way to achieve the goal was to show force, make demands, and use sheer strength to get what they wanted. So, they staged demonstrations, made commando attacks on Turkish enclaves, and tried to invade the sultan's government.

But these actions only gave Hamid an excuse to "curb their zeal" by dealing Armenians a blow he believed would cause them once and for all to give up their idea of liberation. The massacres he ordered annihilated some three hundred thousand of our people between 1894 and 1896.

The occupation of the Ottoman Bank to which Haroutiun referred was in 1896 and led to the sultan's murdering eight thousand Armenians in Constantinople as reprisal. The occupation was by a small group of Armenian zealots hoping to arouse Christian nations in Europe to take action in behalf of the Armenian people. They seized the bank, barricaded themselves inside, and succeeded in holding it against Turkish police and military forces. They gave up only after officials of foreign embassies persuaded them that the longer they held out, the more Armenians who would die, and guaranteed them safe conduct to a post in western Europe.

Other than that, however, during those three dark years the European nations lent no help to the Armenian cause and did nothing to curb the appalling massacres. Then, finally, three influences brought the butchery to an end:

1. Turkish frustration from steel-willed armed resistance by brave Armenians in parts of the empire
2. Simmering turmoil among the Turks themselves that increasingly was festered by Hamid's despotic rule over his own people

3. At long last, a warning by European powers that they would intervene if the killing didn't stop.

—A Disturbing Omen!—

Two years after I had been sent to the Sis orphanage, my mother had a terrible dream. In it the body of my brother Boghos, torn to bits and placed on a platter, was brought before her. With unimaginable fear, she wakened, weeping. The sight of both of her eyes was gone, and she became gravely ill!

At her request, my older brother Khacher came to the orphanage during the summer recess and took me back to the village to see her.

When we arrived, my mother placed her hand on my forehead. "Hovhannes!" she called out. She embraced me and tears streamed down her face. How sad it was to see her in this condition.

For a month, I remained with her. When it was time for me to return to the orphanage, she gave me some sound advice: "My son, thanks to God that I fulfilled my vow before my death. When you were an infant, you became sick. I promised God that if He would spare your life, I would send you to school for an education so that you could serve Him wisely and serve the Armenian people as well. God heard my tearful plea, and I, before dying, have been able to send you to the orphanage and in that way to keep my vow.

"Therefore, my son, do not forget your mother's last counsel. Do not forget the pure waters of our village, those waters you drank and in which I bathed you to cure you of your fever. Do not forget our graves, where your father was buried two weeks before your birth and in which I, too, will be buried. You were baptized in the font of the Saint Asdvadzadzin Church and you were named after your father. Do not forget your ancestry that was begot through the blood of heroes. Do not forget the Armenian people of which you are a product. Go back to school. Gain an education, grow up, become learned, and return to your native hearth to serve your people."

Sniveling, I returned to the orphanage.

Seven years later, the heart-rending, terrible dream my mother had was to turn real! In 1909, in the great slaughter of Cilicia, my brother Boghos was to become a victim of the "Grey Wolves" on the battlefield.

—A Period of Change—

The orphanage in Sis was closed in 1901, and all the students had to leave. The reason given was that Krikor Shatsian, the benefactor, had been killed in Baku.

When I reached Osmaniye on my return, the local priest did not let me go to our village. Instead, he made me his temporary assistant. I began to teach, young as I was, in the Armenian school of Osmaniye.

When I received a few coins as my first wages, I immediately bought some candy and helva and sent them to my mother and brothers by a muleteer. Later I was told they were overjoyed by my having sent them the gift from the proceeds of my first gainful occupation. My mother, still sick in bed, said, "I fulfilled my vow by sending your brother to school, and now we are enjoying the fruit of his labor. Now I can die in peace."

The fact is that she did die not long after that, at age

thirty-nine. To the very day, it was one year from the night she had had that terrible dream!

When the school closed for the summer recess, I went to our village. The first thing I did was go to my mother's grave. I kissed it and shed some tears over it.

In order to comfort me, the Mugrditchian clan gathered together. They represented six or seven families. Included were my ninety-year-old uncle Asadour, the family of my paternal grandfather, grandchildren, and my two brothers, Khacher and Boghos. They tried in every way to console me, but I could not sleep nights.

One night after I went to bed, I could hear my two brothers talking. They thought I was asleep. They decided to have me marry, even at my immature age, to keep me in the village. That night I had no sleep at all. I thought and thought about the matter. There was only one decision I could reach. That was to spare no effort to go to the city of Aintab (now Gaziantep) and continue my education. I was determined to fulfill my mother's vow.

When I was in the Sis orphanage, two men had come from Aintab to be ordained as priests. After the ordination, they remained at the monastery for forty days of vigil and preparation. They told me there were many schools in Aintab, including an orphanage, where boys of my age were getting a higher education. Aintab was definitely where I must go.

In the morning, before my brothers left for their work, I told them of my decision, reminding them of our mother's vow. They tried to persuade me not to go, saying they had a girl in Beshig Kertme ready to marry me. I told them my mind and heart were set. My brother Boghos, seeing how eager I was, said quite emotionally, "I'll take you. We'll also take along some tobacco and cover our costs."

Our villagers, including our clan, cultivated tobacco of high quality, and it sold well. Muleteers came from Aintab to buy the product and sell it at great profit in the city. They were, however, circumventing the payment of tax.

So, the next morning my two brothers loaded our donkey with a bundle of tobacco, and sat me on top of it. Boghos and I went off to join a mule caravan.

Upon our arrival in Aintab, we stopped at a khan (inn) in the Arasan marketplace. That was where I would stay until I could find a place to live.

It didn't take long for Boghos to sell the tobacco we had brought. He gave me some of the money from the proceeds. I thanked him and told him I would be all right on my own. Suddenly a policeman appeared! Seeing that Boghos was an outsider, he was going to arrest him! I ran over to the policeman and offered him a few coins to let my brother go. Boghos quickly put a few coins in the policeman's hand and took off immediately to avoid further difficulty.

Right away, I went to the huge, newly built church of Aintab to see Vahan Kahana Giuldalian. I had met him in Sis when he was ordained a priest. Fortunately, I found him, and through him, Samuel Keoshgerian, who had been one of the seminarians at the Sis monastery and with whom I had become well acquainted. He now was a teacher in the Armenian school of Aintab.

Then began an exceedingly anxious period of trying to get into a school. Mr. Keoshgerian did everything he could to pave the way for me, but it was a difficult task. A fine and patriotic man, he later was ordained a priest in the Baghche parish, being named Der Mesrob Kahana Keoshgerian.

I spent many days appealing to priests to place me in an Armenian school. My meager funds were nearly depleted. Each day I ate only grapes because they were so cheap; I was getting thin from not having enough food.

One Sunday after the service of the Divine Liturgy, I was sitting meekly near the door of a room in which the priests were discussing me.

The church sexton, Yeghia Emmi, who knew of my problem, was also at the door, waiting impatiently for the meeting to finish. Finally, he burst into the room and shouted, "Shame on you!" Then he took me by the arm and said, "I have one son. Let there be two."

My surprise gave way to the sudden relief I felt. How happy I was to go with him to his home. He introduced me to his wife and two children. And smiling at me, he said, "Tomorrow, I'll enroll you in the Nersisian National School. Don't worry about a thing, my boy."

This humble sexton was at the same time steward of the Nersisian School. He was an upstanding, patriotic man. During the 1895 massacres, he had served as a messenger, traveling between Aintab, Iskenderoun, Marash, and Zeitun.

The next day he took me to the Nersisian School and presented me to the teaching staff. After being tested, I was admitted to the highest class in the school. It was my good fortune to have found a father who also was my patron.

—New Experiences—

The school was in a two-story building constructed in 1860 with money bequeathed in the will of Aintab native, Deacon Hovsep Ashjian, of the Brotherhood of St. James of Jerusalem. Over the years, many of the students became seminarians at the St. James Seminary of Jerusalem. We studied Armenian, Armenian history, Turkish, arithmetic, and music.

I was quite weak in arithmetic. Kind soul that he was, Joseph Niziblian, my teacher, would call me in during the midday recess. Sacrificing his deserved rest, he would explain to me the various rules of arithmetic. His help in this way made it possible for me to make up for my weakness and complete that study.

But that wasn't all. When school was out, he would give me a book, saying, "On your way home, leave this book at my house."

This patriotic family lived at the upper end of the Balikle marketplace. I passed it as I walked home to Yeghia Emmi's house, which was quite far away. With the book in my hand, I would walk along, and Niziblian would not be far behind me. As I approached his house, he would catch up with me, take me by the other hand, and lead me inside. We would have our evening meal together, after which I would go on home. This benevolent action by my teacher inspired and developed in me an inextinguishable and unyielding feeling of humanitarianism that would remain with me always. Blessed be the memory of this kind man.

Blessed be also the memory of Philipos Hoja Sarkisian, teacher of Armenian history at the school. The son-in-law of the very wealthy Nazar Effendi, Philipos Hoja, a native of Zeitun, was a graduate of the Nubar Shahnazarian

School of Constantinople. Often he would invite me to dinner at his family's house, always a most enjoyable and instructive occasion. Through his leadership, the Christian Society was formed in the Armenian Apostolic Church. Its purpose was to reawaken the desire for consecrated service. Three of its members were sent to the regions of Amanus for dedicated service.

The people of Aintab held Sunday meetings featuring instructive talks and lectures. Those at the Armenian Apostolic Church were conducted by the Christian Study Group. The Armenian Protestants had their own religious meetings. The Revivalists and Seventh Day Adventists each had theirs. Followers of the latter two groups would gather sometimes in the evenings at members' homes to hear their preachers.

The Gregorian (Armenian Apostolic) people held their gatherings only on Sundays. These were in the Armenian National School. Philipos Hoja was famous as an orator, and after church, crowds would assemble in the Vartanian School to hear him. I always attended these sessions, running from one to another. In the evenings, I would go to meetings of the other religious groups, but I did not believe passively all I heard. I endeavored to use my mind and reasoning powers to broaden my knowledge and become well versed in the different ideas.

The Armenian Religious Society, knowing the kind care Yeghia Emmi was providing me despite his relative poverty, decided to lighten his burden. They arranged to have shoes and clothing made for me. And on Sundays, taking turns, they would invite me to their homes for dinner. The generosity of the Armenians of Aintab was never to be forgotten.

And Aintab itself was an outstanding city. In all of

Turkey, it followed Constantinople as being the best in education, culture, and progressiveness. Armenians would come from all over to this hearth of enlightenment to raise their intellectual levels. But alas, the hopes of the Armenian people were to be drowned in the flood of innocent Armenian blood shed in more tragedies that were to befall us!

—Another Move—

I completed my studies at the Nersisian School at the end of June 1904. I was anxious to continue my education at some other school. But where?

The Aintab Religious Society and Yeghia Emmi conferred on the matter. They considered sending me to the Armash Seminary. The political situation during those days of the Red Sultan (Abdul Hamid II) was extremely bad, however. Traveling to remote areas was dangerous, especially for young men. Passports were required even to go from villayet (state) to villayet. But I was not registered in the government rolls. I was using the name of the registered boy in our village. I was afraid to use my real name.

The Religious Society, after a long meeting, decided to send me to the monastery school in Jerusalem. I would go ostensibly on a pilgrimage to the Holy Land so that the government officials wouldn't be suspicious; people were free to go on religious pilgrimages. I would go with a caravan to Baghche. I would have a letter to the vicar there, Der Vahan Kahana, asking that he take care of providing me with a passport. Then he was to send me to Iskenderoun where a businessman, H. Khachadourian of

Aintab, a member of the Religious Society, was living. A separate letter to this gentleman would ask that he send me on, by ship, to Jerusalem.

It was difficult to part from such a warm and friendly environment, especially from that patriot Yeghia Emmi, my second father and protector, and his family, who had made possible my studies at the Nersisian School.

The caravan reached Baghche after being soaked in a heavy downpour. I stayed at the home of my aunt (mother's sister), a midwife. Der Vahan Kahana lived there on the first floor.

My aunt introduced me to that venerable priest. On reading the letter I gave him, he immediately sent me to our village to have me bring back to him the name of someone who was registered in the government rolls. I no longer could use the name Vartevar.

Our village priest, Der Hovhannes, also the village head, found a boy who was officially registered. His name was Movses. I was given papers with that name and returned to Baghche. Then I went with Vahan Kahana to the chief of passports, Asaf Effendi, whose office was in the government building.

I was fortunate that Vahan Kahana had a good name and, being highly esteemed, was influential in all the region of Amanus. Asaf Effendi studied the papers, looked me over carefully, and said in Turkish, "The age written here is eleven, but this boy appears to be fifteen or sixteen years old."

Der Vahan got red in the face and said, "Asaf Effendi, don't stir things up. You'll get into difficulty." Asaf Effendi blushed and erased the entry, changing the year of birth to show me as sixteen. Then he gave me an official passport. We thanked him and happily I put the passport into my pocket.

The next day I headed for Iskenderoun. After arriving, I went to H. Khachadourian and gave him the letter the Religious Society of Aintab had furnished me. He kindly took me into his house as his guest until a ship going to Jaffa (now Tel Aviv) arrived.

While I was there, another boy arrived and stayed with us. His name was Sarkis Topjian and he was from Aintab. But he had no official passport. He, too, was going to Jerusalem. How could he without a passport? He would need one to board the ship.

Khachadourian worked it out when the ship arrived. He arranged with the pilot of the tender to have Sarkis lie hidden on the bottom of the tender. I threw my blanket over him, and by some careful maneuvering when we got to the ship, we were able to get him on board.

A few days later, we arrived in Jaffa and went directly to the Armenian monastery. The chief abbot received us and put us on the train to Jerusalem. There we were placed in the first grade of Saint James Seminary.

–III–

A Career Begins

The superintendent of the seminary school in Jerusalem was Der Garabed Vartabed Mikaelian. We studied Armenian, Turkish, French, ethics, history, physics, theology, music, and physical education.

Our theology teacher, Der Nerses Vartabed Kharakhanian, later was ordained a bishop and became primate of Mush. Another teacher, Hovhannes Eolmezian, was elected catholicos in 1908.

Dirouni Hagop Emmi of Ourfa was our night watchman. Like a loving father, he took care of us at night. We also had a mayrabed (mother superior), who played the role of mother. She took great pains to keep us healthy. I'll never forget the preventive drink she made from boiled rose petals. Our cook was Mourad, of Marash, who prepared tasty dishes for us.

And we had a physician, Dr. Vahan. One day when we were playing soccer my heel was thrown out of joint. My companions carried me back to the school. Dr. Vahan could do nothing for it. But our night watchman was a former sunukji (native chiropractor). On seeing my condition and the doctor's inability to do anything about it, he came up to me with a smile. He examined my foot. In one sharp movement, he put the bones in place, then wrapped the foot tightly. Smiling again, he said, "My boy, you must not play soccer for a year." I abided faithfully by his advice, and to this day, I have never had any trouble with the foot.

Professor Aleksan Bezjian, the author of our physics textbook, visited Jerusalem in 1906. He came to our classroom, observed our work, and expressed great pleasure with it. His praise and encouragement were testimony to the excellent instruction we were fortunate to receive at the seminary.

During our second year, Der Bedros Vartabed Sarajian was designated school supervisor. One day he called me into his office, gave me the key to our fine library, and named me librarian. I was delighted and spent my free time there reading many books, sometimes, in secret, even forbidden books. One work I chanced upon was a booklet on hypnotism by Kazanjian. I found the subject fascinating, so much so that I studied it over and over. In time, I actually found myself to be quite proficient in that art. And this resulted in an amusing incident.

It was the custom on every New Year's Eve to have a party attended by the supervisor, the teaching staff, and the students. At the party in 1908, Father Sarajian began hypnotizing several of the boys, putting them into a deep sleep and planting in their minds the idea of celibacy. He was using this sly way to promote and strengthen celibacy as an institution of the church.

When my turn came, he looked deeply and meaningfully into my eyes, trying to subject me to his will. Because I knew hypnotism, I began to develop a firm resistance,

26

however. Soon the supervisor tired from his failure to overcome my stubbornness. His eyes started to water. A teacher from Constantinople, Ajemian, began to laugh loudly, sensing that I knew the art. And all the students also began to laugh hilariously. It was the highlight of the party!

Easter also was a special occasion. On this holy day, all the members of the St. James Brotherhood of Jerusalem and all the seminarians were permitted to dine together in the refectory, under the presidency of the patriarch. The purpose was to show there was no discrimination between the ordained members of the brotherhood and the seminarians, that equality existed among all ranks, high and low. During the meal, absolute silence prevailed. Only the voice of the deacon at the lectern could be heard reading selections from the Haysmavourk (annals of the lives and works of the saints). It was a moving, impressive event.

During our years of study at the seminary, we often went up Mount Tabor (Ascension Hill). A monastery built by a Russian czar stood there. Alongside was a high tower that served as a belfry, and we always climbed to the top. The bell was so large that eight to ten of us could put our heads inside of it at one time and sing patriotic songs. Next to the belfry was another building. On it a mosaic inscription with Armenian letters said, as I remember it: "In memory of Shoushan, daughter of the Great Vartan." There once had been an Armenian monastery at this location; early on, Armenians had built more than seventy monasteries and churches in Jerusalem and the surrounding area.

—My Own Identity—

A momentous occurrence took place in 1908. Turkey promulgated a new constitution in July of that year. It proclaimed freedom, justice, equality, and fraternity. The news excited all the people. Filled with joy, they poured out into the streets everywhere.

In Jerusalem, Turk, Armenian, and Arab orators followed one another on platforms, praising the declaration and filling the air with words of jubilation. The leader of the military band was an Armenian, and he had the band go around playing Armenian songs, even "Pamp, Vorodan" (a military march).

To join in the celebration, the brotherhood of the Armenian monastery, the superintendent of the seminary, and all the students decided to form a procession. The day before it was to take place, my teacher, Hovhannes Eolmezian, asked me to prepare a talk on behalf of the seminarians. I felt honored to be given this assignment.

The next day, our procession started out at the courtyard of Saint James and proceeded to David's Tower toward the center of the city. A platform had been erected on high ground on the west side of the street. I was directed there to make my speech.

The crowd standing before me was immense. I was surprised that I was not nervous. In my talk, I praised the Young Turks and their Committee of Union and Progress for having succeeded in getting the constitution promulgated. I compared it to the French Constitution that promised equality and fraternity to all citizens. The crowd applauded thunderously, including the Arabs, who had not understood a word.

Who could imagine that less than a year later, in April

1909, more than thirty thousand of our compatriots in Cilicia would be massacred by these same Young Turks I was praising?

These men were determined to demonstrate that the "new" Turkey they were forging was under their absolute control. Their impression was that the Armenians in Cilicia weren't fully recognizing this and needed a vivid reminder that the Turks were the rulers, Armenians the subjects. Lost in the horrible slaughter were all the adult males of our Mugrditchian clan!

In the eleventh century, large numbers of Armenians fleeing Byzantine persecution had established a new Armenian kingdom in Cilicia on the Mediterranean coast. Due to its strategic location for trade, the kingdom flourished for centuries as an independent Armenian nation, only to become ultimately part of an expanding Ottoman Empire. That long-ago escape from persecution was not destined to endure forever.

My graduation approached. I was in constant anguish, wondering how long I would have to continue using a false name. I wanted so much for the school diploma to be inscribed with my own name.

Another concern that kept parading through my mind was the matter of celibacy. I was not a subdeacon. Graduates were to be ordained archdeacons. And, according to the rules of that time, archdeacons had to enter the celibate priesthood later. This was something I felt I did not want to do.

Finally, I decided to call again for help from Der Vahan Stepanian of Baghche, who had made it possible for me to enter the Sis orphanage school under another boy's name. I wrote him a letter. In it, I asked for his assistance in getting a birth certificate bearing my real name and surname. Also, I asked for his counsel on the celibacy question.

His response brought me joy that had no bounds. Quickly, I had the desired birth certificate from him. And concerning celibacy, he wrote that the apostle had advised, "Let him bear it who can."

Immediately I went to our superintendent and showed him the birth certificate and the letter. He, too, was overjoyed that a student who had gone under two false names for so long and had traveled from city to city now had proof of his real name and surname. He explained the whole matter to the teaching staff, and thereafter I was called by my right name, Hovhannes Mugrditchian.

—On to Teaching—

Twelve of us were graduated from the seminary on June 12, 1909. When it was proposed that I be ordained an archdeacon and later become a celibate priest, I declined, adding, however, that I was grateful for the education I had been given. I was ready to serve my people and go wherever I might be sent. Soon I had my first assignment. It was in Jaffa, to teach in what was to be a new Armenian school. At the same time, I was designated accountant for the monastery where the school would be located.

After arriving in Jaffa, I started work at once. There was a suitable building on the grounds of the monastery, and we converted it into a school. Because the Armenian population in that city was small, fewer than twenty children were enrolled. While getting the school under way, I also was busy working with the monastery to put its income-producing stores under accounting control. My early days of struggling to learn arithmetic often came back to me, and I now was especially thankful for the help I had received.

The next year two unfortunate occurrences rocked the school. First, the superintendent, Yeretsian, was stabbed by a Turk while walking in the marketplace one day. He died before reaching a hospital. The second involved the man who replaced the murdered superintendent. He was old and had little intellectual capability. At dinner in the refectory one evening I noticed a bandage on one of his thumbs. He said it was only a small wound and that he had put medicine on it. The "medicine" turned out to be poisonous; he died four days later. Telian Vartabed, far more knowledgeable and competent, was sent from Constantinople to replace him.

Despite these upsetting events, things went well at the school. I even received an invitation from a rich family in Zile to go there and teach. But they had in mind that I would marry their daughter Santoukhd. I had met them a year earlier when they had come on a pilgrimage to Jerusalem and had visited our school.

The invitation was declined quickly. A rich family in Jaffa also had suggested marriage to their daughter. Though it was comforting to be viewed favorably as a prospective son-in-law, I was not ready to take on a wife.

In due course, through my close friendship with a Jaffa artisan named Kevorkian and his family, another teaching opportunity opened for me, this time in Sis.

After the massacres in Cilicia, Catholicos Sahag planned to open a new seminary school in the Sis monastery. He began to seek out instructors. My friend Kevorkian recommended me to be teacher-director at the new facility. The next thing I knew, a letter came from

Catholicos Sahag inviting me to serve in that capacity. I could not decline this offer to go where, for a time, I had spent my boyhood days imbued with a desire for consecrated study.

Immediately I went to then patriarchal vicar Archbishop Drtad Balian to request his permission to leave. I explained that I wanted to go because it was in Cilicia that all of the adult males of my family had been massacred and the survivors were in dire need of help. He understood and wished me success.

–IV–

Back Home

There was a serious need for teachers. In Adana, on my way to Sis, the local primate wanted me to remain there to teach in the Apkarian Armenian School. I felt sorry about not being able to oblige him, but I knew my right place was in Sis.

It was a joy to be back where I had come years before as a poor, lonely boy seeking to fulfil my mother's vow that I get an education. What pleasant reunions there were with friends and acquaintances from those earlier days!

Right away I set to work organizing the school. It was a challenge, but with much help from colleagues at the monastery, things fell into place. We had fine teachers and excellent students. By the end of the first year, we could look back and feel a real sense of accomplishment.

The year was not without anxiety, however. It was 1912 and the Balkan wars had started.

In accordance with provisions of the new Ottoman constitution, all males of military age had to enlist. Graduates of higher education could not be taken into the military services, but my credentials had been delayed in arriving from Constantinople. Each day, Turkish officials would come to the monastery to enlist me, and it was getting increasingly difficult for the catholicos to keep them from doing so.

Naturally, I was deeply worried, wondering why the needed paper showing my education had not arrived and when would it come. In the midst of all this worry, an idea came to me. I had a pupil named Avedis. He was an uncommonly bright, healthy boy from Deortyol. I thought he would be a good candidate for using the power of hypnotism to seek an answer to my problem.

Avedis agreed to let me hypnotize him. I put him into a deep trance and asked whether he could see any document with my name on it. He answered, "I see a paper folded in two. One side has your name on it in Armenian, the other in Turkish. Both sides have a large seal. The number 1050 is written on it." I then asked him how many days away the paper was. He replied that it would arrive in two days. I ordered him to awaken at the count of five, kissed him on the forehead, and thanked him happily.

The experiment was a success. Two days later the paper was in my hands. When an official came again to enlist me, I showed it to him. He read the Turkish part and looked at the great seals, one of the Armenian patriarchate, the other of the Turkish government. I was spared from military service.

Not long after that, I had a most pleasant visitor. Yeghia Emmi, the sexton of the Aintab church who had done so much for me as provider-father many years before, learned that I was in Sis. After traveling five to six days, he came to see me. It was a happy reunion. He stayed with me for a week. When he left, I pressed into his hands two gold Ottoman coins. We parted with warm wishes for each other and the hope that we again would get together. We could not foresee what lay ahead to make it our last visit.

In another period of anxiety at Sis, I again called on hypnotism. An epidemic of cholera broke out, with ten to fifteen persons dying daily. From the high walls of our monastery, we sadly could see the burials taking place. The infection even invaded the monastery. Aware of the serious danger, I began self-hypnosis. Every night before retiring, I would take a glass of water in my hand, and with deep faith, I would say repeatedly, "I am very young. The cholera cannot affect me." Then I would drink the water and go to sleep. I remained untouched by the sickness.

During my first year at the monastery school, I put off doing anything about a leak in the roof, which kept getting worse. One day I got a ladder and climbed up to see what was needed for repair. While standing there, I noticed two figures, a mother and daughter, approaching on horseback along the road. The closer they came, the less I could take my eyes off the daughter, who appeared to be about twelve years old.

They stopped at the school. I quickly learned in speaking to them that they were Mrs. Ovsanna Panosian and her daughter, Beatrice. They had come from their home in Aintab to visit Beatrice's brother, who was a student at the school. I was delighted to receive them.

The Panosians were a highly respected family in Aintab. Mr. Panosian, who died when Beatrice was five years old, had been a successful leather merchant. Ovsanna had a beautiful singing voice and was in demand as a soloist.

Beatrice, very bright as well as attractive, attended an all-girl school. They had a large home, and relatives lived there with them, each having a separate room.

During their visit, it didn't take long to sense in both my mind and my heart that I had found my future wife. Here was a lovely girl whose interest in education had given her a depth of knowledge far beyond her years. How pleasant it was to talk with her, indeed just to be with her.

It was my good fortune that Ovsanna, a charming and friendly woman, invited me to have dinner at their home on a weekend after they returned to Aintab. This was a most happy occasion on which I had an opportunity to spend more time with Beatrice. And the good fortune extended to receiving further invitations to dinner.

Although Beatrice appeared to enjoy our times together, she made it clear she wanted to continue her education and was not ready to be a wife. (I was by no means her only suitor.) Ovsanna, however, had other ideas. She kept telling her that because of the Turkish massacres, she must marry in order to have the protection of a man. Finally, Beatrice gave in, saying she would marry the suitor with the best education. I was the lucky winner.

Toward the end of my second year as teacher and director of the monastery school, I felt a longing for my birthplace. The needs of hundreds of orphans in miserable state filled me with anguish. I kept thinking of my mother's last words to me before she died, "Gain an education, grow up, become learned, and return to your native hearth to serve your people."

The longing led me to resign from my position at the end of the year and leave for our village.

—Peril in Bapajle—

Upon returning to my birthplace in 1912, I took up residence at the home of a relative, Jaji Avedikian, who set aside a room for me. My plan was to open an Armenian school as soon as possible.

The village church had been set afire and destroyed during the Cilician massacre of 1909. The priest had been killed along with 165 others. Residents of the village had been left leaderless and unprotected. A kahana had been sent from Marash to take care of the people's religious needs by going to their homes.

A new church was under construction on a high, open plot of land. The villagers, widows and orphans included, were working together to erect it. A secret vault was being built into the wall above the main altar. This was to hold weapons for self-defense if needed in the future; the recent past had served as a lesson.

A room next to the balcony of the church would house the school. As a temporary measure, we used the home of my mother's sister, Ebeje Khatoun, for classes. As a helper, I had the son of Vartevar Keshishian Der Ghevont, a leader among the survivors.

Meanwhile, at the request of a group of young men who miraculously had escaped the massacre, and to satisfy my own desire, I began to train them secretly in techniques I had learned in the use of weapons, marksmanship, and military tactics. It was crucial that the surviving villagers be on guard at all times. Unfortunately, enemies found out about this.

The most ruthless butcher of Armenians in the villages of Amanus in the 1909 Cilician massacre was known as Black Hasan. He had been sentenced to 101 years in exile on Rhodes Island, but later was released, filled with hate and vengeance. I found out that his son had formed a small band of brigands and that they were out to get me because of what I was doing to train our young men.

Meanwhile, Beatrice and I were married on January 25, 1913. The girl who had ridden into my life on horseback became a partner to whom I have been devoted every day since.

Three days after our wedding terror struck! On the way home after dark, I was sprung upon suddenly. The attackers hit me on the head and tried to throw me down to my knees. Black Hasan's son started squeezing my head wound. I struggled fiercely and managed to hit him in the groin with my fist. The quick pain he felt caused him to release his hold on my head. I broke away and ran to get my brother Khacher.

Although one of my eyes was closed from the bleeding on my head, we armed ourselves, found the hoodlums, and attacked them. Other villagers joined us. The villains ran and took cover in the darkness of the night.

Some of our boys immediately went to Baghche and informed our close family friend Krikor Koudoulian about the incident. At the time, he was teaching in the Baghche Armenian school. He informed the local government the next morning. That same day, Black Hasan's son went to the marketplace in Baghche to buy gunpowder. Police who were there saw that the clothing under his right arm was bloody. He was arrested and taken to Osmaniye to be tried.

It was necessary for me to be present at the trial. I traveled from Lapajle to Osmaniye by horse, using a zigzag route that took me six hours. I wanted to avoid falling into any trap the attackers might have tried to set for me.

Black Hasan maneuvered to get his son released through offering bribes to officials. The governor was an Albanian and despised Turkish brigands. I was told that Black Hasan brought a tin tub filled with butter to him as a bribe to get the son free. This is what the governor was reported to have said to him: "You brought this butter to persuade me to intercede in the trial and free your son. With this attempted bribe you have established the fact that the main criminal was your son." After a long trial, the judge gave his verdict: fifteen years imprisonment.

Some time later, the son, with the help of other prisoners, broke out of jail in the middle of the night. The guard on duty was Hovhannes of Zeitun. Three times he called "Stop!" The criminal kept going. With a single shot Black Hasan's son was slain. An Armenian was avenged by an Armenian.

—A Distinguished Visitor—

In 1913, when Sahag, the catholicos of Cilicia, was visiting in the area of Zeitun and Marash, I was informed that he would come to our village on the Feast of Vartavar (Transfiguration) fourteen weeks after Easter. He was to be accompanied by Shahe Vartabed Kasparian of Aintab whose father, Hoja Kaspar, was my music teacher when I was at school in Aintab.

The people of Lapajle arranged a fine reception. A group of young men under Sarkis Avedikian rode their horses out to greet the catholicos. The reception committee had slaughtered lambs for a big banquet under a huge walnut tree in front of my mother's brother's home. The guests drank Sutma Pourna, our mineral water, and were highly pleased with its taste. The festivity was reminiscent of the old days when there were great celebrations on religious feasts.

At the affair, I made a plea to Catholicos Sahag about the future welfare of our newly opened village school. I presented a large number of orphans who were in dire need of daily food and Armenian education. The catholicos was deeply moved and responded by promising to set up an annual budget of thirty-eight gold Ottomans to cover our school costs, thereby assuring that the school would continue to operate. He blessed all present and wished us success in our undertaking. He then left for Sis. This great leader's visit brought unforgettable joy to all the people of our village.

But my work in Lapajle soon was to be cut short!

My aunt served as a midwife in the village. Often, Turkish residents of other villages would come to get her to aid in births. One day she was taken to the village of Nohoudli for that purpose. While there, she overheard Turkish women talking about Black Hasan, organizer of the terrible 1909 massacre in the Armenian villages of Amanus. It appeared that he was planning to have Khacher and me killed. When my aunt returned, she hurried to warn me, advising that I leave the village at once.

By coincidence, the chairman of the town council of Osmaniye, Garabed Daghestanlian, Effendi, had come to ask me to move to Osmaniye and open an Armenian school there. After a long discussion with our village kahana and other leaders, the decision was that I would go there. The kahana promised that he would help Vartevar Keshishian's son keep the Lapajle school in operation.

Thus, in September 1913, we moved to Osmaniye. I

went to work right away to open a school in the one suitable building. It was being used for religious services because the Osmaniye church had been destroyed by fire in the 1909 massacre. Beatrice would be teaching with me in the new school.

—A Tragic Loss—

My brother Khacher had become a terror to the Turks of the Kara Edigli village. Although this posed great danger to him, he didn't let it stop him.

It was his custom to go a few times each year to hunt boars in Karagedik, on the shore of the Ceyhan River, where my father's sister lived with her family. On October 11, 1913, he went to Baghche to buy gunpowder and bullets for one of these hunts. The storekeeper, a Turk, asked him the reason for the purchase. Khacher told him that he planned to go hunting in Karagedik.

That was fatal! Black Hasan's men, who were always after Khacher, heard about it and plotted to ambush him on the road to Karagedik. They took up a position behind trees at the side of the road as it passed through the Sazartepid Forest. As the incident was reconstructed, when Khacher, on horseback, reached that point, the men treacherously shot him in the back. From the enormity of the wounds, he had to have died instantly. His horse, running off, turned up at a farm belonging to our relatives. They kept their animals there during the winter because the weather was milder in that area.

My uncle's grandson, Haroutiun Mugrditchian, recognized the horse and realized something must have happened to Khacher. Greatly concerned, he and others left hurriedly to search for him along the road to Karagedik. With shock and horror, they came upon his bloodied, limp body lying on the road. They brought the body to the farm and got word of the murder to government officials in Baghche, as well as to our friends there.

Our dear friend Krikor Koudoulian wired me in Osmaniye. The wire arrived at our house on a Sunday when I was in church. Beatrice received it and was so distraught in getting the terrible news that she became bedridden.

It would be difficult to express fully the combined sorrow and anger that engulfed me when I, too, was stunned by reading the message. Six years before, my brother Boghos had been slain on the battlefield. Now Khacher was gone. What an awful waste of young manhood hate had wrought through the centuries!

Khacher's body was taken to the Osmaniye morgue. With Dr. Vahan Vanlian, the only government physician in the city, and some policemen, I went there. What a sad experience it was. The doctor examined the wounds on the body, then went to make a written report to the Osmaniye government. After that, we took the body to Lapajle and laid Khacher to rest alongside my parents. Now his wife was a widow with three children. I gave her all the money I had in my pocket to take care of immediate family needs and returned home. There I was shocked to find that my wife Beatrice, who was five months pregnant, had suffered a miscarriage from the extreme emotional stress caused by the killing. She had lost a male fetus.

It turned out that the leader of the group of killers lived in Karagedik and was known to the pastor of our relatives there. The pastor gave me the criminal's name and address, and I immediately informed Dr. Vanlian. Together, we gave the information to local government authorities. Police quickly arrested the murderer and brought him to Osmaniye.

It was a rule of the time that the government physician had to give each prisoner a medical examination for the protection of other prisoners. Our patriotic doctor, taking advantage of the opportunity, injected a strong poison into the killer, advising that to avoid infection no one should go near the man for a few days. The next day the murderer began to scream in intense pain. He ran out of the prison building into the yard, fell down, and died. It was on a Sunday. During church services, Hagop, one of our students—he was the doctor's son—came and whispered in my ear, "Congratulations, Effendi, your brother's killer is dead." Our loyal and esteemed physician had avenged us.

—Dark Clouds Forming—

In July of the following year, 1914, the summer recess at school gave me an opportunity to pursue a strong desire to learn more about the families who had founded our village of Lapajle. Descendants were living in Zeitun, Furnuz, and Gaban (Geben). Accordingly, Beatrice and I went to Marash, planning to go on to Zeitun and surrounding villages.

Hardly had we rented a room when the kahana and other acquaintances asked why we had come. They advised us not to venture out of the city, explaining that war-related conditions made traveling very dangerous. They told us that the leaders of Zeitun already had been taken into custody and jailed. We realized it was wise to take their advice and give up going to Zeitun and surroundings. Only a few days later, July 21, 1914, the Ottoman government issued a mobilization order ("saferberlik").

We returned to Osmaniye with difficulty. Mounting events were a portent of dire things to come. Ironically, right after we reached home a letter arrived from the parish council in Cyprus inviting me to teach in the Cyprus Armenian School. At the same time, I had a letter from a former classmate, Raphael Geokjian, urging me to go at once to Cyprus. Unfortunately, I had to decline. I could not go back on a previous commitment I had made to the parish council in Osmaniye.

– V –

The Armenian Golgotha

In August 1914, Germany and Russia were at war. The Turks decided to side with Germany. In November, the Ottoman government entered the war alongside the Germans against not only Russia, but England and France as well. Large forces of soldiers were being transported to reinforce the fronts at Baghdad and the Suez Canal. Osmaniye was on the Baghdad railway, and the Turks placed a large military force in the city for such transportation.

For military needs, the Turkish government began occupying a number of buildings in Osmaniye. They took our Armenian school. A retired Turkish colonel, Asouf Bey, living in Osmaniye, and Abdulla Agha of Adana, both with children in the school, tried to prevent this. But the Turks, who had no schools of their own, ignored them. We had no choice but to use our homes as classrooms.

Conditions worsened in 1915. Armenians of military age were conscripted for Amele Tabouri units (labor battalions). Under the excuse of military necessity, the Turks began to gather up all sorts of supplies, including animals and foodstuffs. In return, they gave receipts supposedly to be repaid after the war. Through caravan muleteers, we learned about the great oppression to which the Armenian people of Zeitun were being subjected. More than seventy-five notables had been arrested and tied together, then taken to Marash where, after suffering insult and ridicule, they were imprisoned. Catholicos Sahag succeeded in having them released from jail, but they were exiled to Deir ez Zor (now Dayraz Zawr), where sure death awaited them in the Syrian desert.

We also were told about a rebellion of twenty-two youths from Zeitun. Under the leadership of a brave lad named Aram Chavoush, they had engaged Turkish soldiers in a fight and had killed some three hundred of them. Immediately after the battle, aided by the darkness of night, they found refuge in the mountains and increased their size by having other young men join them to fight against the Turks.

—Man's Inhumanity—

The forced deportation of Armenians began in April 1915. Deprived of our native homelands of three millennia, we were driven out, group by group, on tortuous trails.

Estimates of the number of deaths that occurred along the way and at final destinations range from three hundred thousand to two million. The strong likelihood is that it did exceed one million. A tragedy of this magnitude provided clear evidence that the genocidal Turks had seized on the war as an excuse to exterminate Armenians as a people.

For years after, however, Turkish leaders persistently,

but unconvincingly, maintained that the deportation was purely a necessary wartime measure on their part. Along with Germany, they were at war with Russia. They claimed that the large Armenian presence in the eastern part of the empire was a threat because of potential Armenian aid to Russia. At the same time, they cited their fear of increased uprisings and disruptions, also a hindrance to the war effort, as the reason for getting the Armenians out of Cilicia.

The Turks erred, however, in thinking that they could exterminate us. They ignored the past history of the Armenian people—the granitelike faith, the instinct for survival, which over centuries had carried us through attacks by Roman, Byzantine, Persian, and Arab despots. Neither Timourlane nor Genghis Khan had succeeded in forcing Armenians to be assimilated or to change faith or to be wiped off the earth. We were the first to embrace Christianity and make it our national religion (in A.D. 301). We had remained, and would continue to be, steadfast in our beliefs. And we would survive.

In Constantinople, the first group to be deported in 1915 comprised 270 clergymen, intellectuals, writers, editors, teachers, deputies, doctors, and attorneys, all of them leaders of the Armenian people. Few would remain alive. Many mercilessly were killed on mountain slopes or in deep valleys during the months following their deportation.

In May, three hundred people from Zeitun were the first group of deportees to arrive in Osmaniye. They were being driven to regions of Konya to be confined to the grim wastes of Karaponar and Sultaniye with the expectation that all would succumb from hunger and thirst. Our local priest, Der Khoren Kahana Kouyoumjian, and I wanted to provide food to these unfortunate souls, but we were threatened and denied the right to see them.

Two friends, Zohrab and Vartkes, arrived from Constantinople in June on their way to exile in Aleppo. The kahana and I tried to go to the railroad station to see them. The station master was an Armenian from Romania. He warned us to be careful. All we could do was say a brief good-bye to them.

The overall commander of the troops stationed in Osmaniye was an Arab. During the first week of July, he called the kahana and me to his office and warned us of the dangerous situation that prevailed, saying candidly that all Armenians were to be deported. He advised me to enlist as a volunteer to avoid deportation, promising that he would put me under his command and assign me to a definite military rank. I appreciated his offer, but there always was the possibility he would be transferred to another post. That would make my future uncertain and could take me from my people. So I declined, thanking him. We exchanged expressions of mutual respect and parted.

For the rebuilding of our church, a good deal of lumber had been stored in an enclosure. One day we saw soldiers chopping up some of the boards for firewood to cook their meals. We wanted to save that lumber and at night began moving it to the enclosed courtyard of a wealthy Greek (Roum) landowner who was one of our friends.

A miscreant, Karekin of Deortyol, informed the police. I was arrested and imprisoned at the police station. The chief of police was a lame Kurd. After hurling profanities and insults at me, he accused me of being an Armenian revolutionary. Then he filled out a two-page indictment subjecting me to a military court.

On learning of this, my mother-in-law, Ovsanna, who then was living with us, went in tears to the governor of Osmaniye. The governor, Asaf Bey, was from Yozgad. When she told him what had happened, he immediately sent one of his assistants to the police station to demand that the police chief and I come at once to his office. Ovsanna was seated next to the governor when we arrived there. The governor read the indictment fully, turned to the police chief, and said emphatically, "I and all the leaders of Osmaniye know this hoja (teacher) better than you do. He is innocent." He tore up the paper and threw it into a wastebasket. Then he turned to me and said, "Hoja Effendi, I'll give you four days. Get ready. You will be deported to Aleppo with your family."

My mother-in-law and I were shocked! But we knew we had to accept the inevitable.

—*Desperate Journey*—

July 20, 1915, was the date of our forced departure from Osmaniye. Taking only such essentials as clothes and light blankets, the four of us—Beatrice, our infant daughter Koharig, who was just a few months old, my mother-in-law, and I—were on a train with other deportees. We naively believed what government officials had told us: that we would be returning home in a few months. How foolish it was to think we would be safe while we were gone. We had no awareness that the death sentence had been pronounced for all Armenians.

The train went to Islahiye, then to Katma. At Katma, we were joined by Krikor Goekjian, Effendi of Baghche. And from Yanuk Degerman, my father's sister and her family arrived with their children. All told, more than twenty thousand deportees from different areas were massed there.

Frightening news soon passed through the crowds. We heard that strict orders had come that all of us were to be sent without delay to desert death points Rasiulia and Deir ez Zor. The word was that Turkish-organized Kurds, Cherkezes, and Chechens were waiting in these localities like butchers to spill Armenian blood!

Krikor Effendi and I, discussing the situation in huddled anxiety, resolved that, at any cost, we must escape to Aleppo that night, feeling we would be safer there. We carefully organized a group of seven families, succeeded in bribing the police to let us go secretly, and set off after dark.

It was a painful trek. In utter silence, we had to proceed with extreme caution, alert to the slightest sign or sound of danger. Nor could we rest for long at any point. It was imperative that we reach Aleppo in the full of night. Tired and worn, but relieved, we arrived safely and were fortunate to find rooms to rent from Christian Arabs.

Before long, we settled down in rooms in the northern part of the city among Aziz Arab Christians. Now it was a matter of what to do next.

My mother-in-law felt we should send a letter to her son, Yeprem Der Boghosian, and inform him of our circumstances. Yeprem was somewhere near Damascus, a soldier with the rank of captain. He once had been a pupil of mine. We wrote the letter to an address she had for him, and I went to the post office to mail it. Hardly had I reached the post office door when I was arrested and taken to a building near the railroad station.

The building, which the French had intended for a hospital but had abandoned before it was completed, was serving as a processing center for Armenians who had been taken into custody on various pretexts. All were to be sent by train to unknown destinations. I knew I had to get out of there somehow.

After thinking about the situation for a while, I reached into my pocket and found a sizable coin. Then I walked over to the guard stationed at the door, slipped the coin into his hand, and told him I badly needed to go outside to urinate. He pocketed the coin and let me go out. I moved away some distance from the door, then began running with all my might. Police started after me, but lost my trail when I rounded a corner. I saw a partially completed building and crawled under a wooden floor. A while later, I saw a carriage coming along the street and ran out in front of it. I asked the driver to take me to the Aziz quarter. He did so by a route skirting the city. I paid him well, happy to have escaped.

Krikor Effendi and I constantly conferred about what we should do. It was dangerous for any of us even to venture out. But we couldn't stay totally confined to the rooms. Then one day we heard that a manager-steward from the village of Jib Ghabsha near the city of Bab had come to Aleppo looking for people to work in the fields. There was a shortage of help because all the young men of the area had been taken into military service. After much effort, we were able to find this steward and make an agreement to serve as farm laborers. Thus all seven families moved to Jib Ghabsha.

—A Hard Winter—

Our living quarters were small huts. Only a few of us were able to do the farm work, but those who could made the best of it, and the steward was pleased with our efforts. Before long, when he found that several of us could read and write, he began to converse with us. And when he learned I had been in Jerusalem, as he had, he began to call me "Haji." A close friendship grew between us. He even gave me a hunting rifle. And he regularly would invite me into his office where we would drink Arabian coffee together.

The steward had a son about seven or eight years of age. The boy developed a severe case of diarrhea and was getting weaker and weaker. I asked for permission to try to cure the boy, and the steward agreed to it. We called his servant, Hasan, into the room and I instructed him to go at once to Aleppo for pomegranates. Hasan returned the same day with them. We ate and enjoyed the pomegranates, but I took the peels and boiled them thoroughly, then fed the liquid to the boy. The next day his diarrhea was gone. The steward told me with joy that I had saved the boy's life. He and his family were so grateful that we always were welcome in their household and I always was greeted with Haji, Haji, Haji!

The winter that year was exceptionally harsh. Never before had there been snowstorms in the Aleppo area. But this winter there were terrible blizzards and freezing weather. One of our group, Kalayj, of Hasan Beyli, died of typhus. We were barely able to bury him in the frozen ground. Living through the cold weeks was an ordeal for all of us, and we were glad to see the spring finally come.

One day, however, the steward, with a sad look on his

face, called me into his office. He said that what he had to tell me grieved him deeply, but he could do nothing about it. A strict order had come out of Constantinople that all Armenians who had taken refuge in the villages of the area were to be exiled to Deir ez Zor. "You will have to look after yourselves from this day forward," he said sadly. "If it were only you, I could take you into my family. But it is impossible to keep seven families. If anyone tries to provide refuge to the deportees, he will be severely punished."

I quickly informed Krikor Goekjian of the terrible news. After thinking about it a while, he had an idea. He said that Papazian, the engineer in charge of the Intilli railway tunnel under construction to link Baghdad and Constantinople, was a friend of his. "Let's get a message to him," Krikor said excitedly. "If it's at all possible, I know he will help us. He can be our escape."

We composed an urgent letter to Papazian. Three young men of our group volunteered to take it to him. They dressed as Kurds in order to avoid being detected as Armenians. Even so, they faced mortal danger, and fully mindful of this, set out to deliver our plea for help.

A week of anxious waiting followed. We wondered and worried whether our three brave messengers had been able to get there. And if they had, what would Papazian's answer be? It was a tense period of praying and hoping for good news.

But what wonderful relief at the end of that week! Our messengers joyfully returned with a document from Papazian. In it he declared that our seven families were specialists, having previously worked on the Intilli tunnel. He stressed there was great need for our services to expedite completion of the construction and how important it was to finish the tunnel quickly in order to transport troops and supplies to Baghdad and the Suez Canal.

A miracle! How thankful we were to Krikor for his idea and to the three young men who had succeeded in their dangerous task. Papazian indeed was proving to be a friend. The document he had prepared extolling our skills was most convincing—even to us! We showed it to the steward and asked him to help us leave for Intilli, a distance of eleven days.

—A Short Reprieve—

With the steward's help, we hired twenty-one camels and a few donkeys for the long journey. One of the camels was for Beatrice and one of the donkeys for her mother. I would travel on foot, carrying our child. Because Beatrice had fallen ill and had lost much of her strength, we tied her to the camel's back to be sure she would not fall off. We could only pray that she would endure the long journey. Through sheer will, she did manage to do so.

We traveled along the Kilis and Kurd Daghi road. Day and night, we came upon bodies of Armenian deportees, swollen and unrecognizable corpses lying beside the road, victims of an inhumanity that knew no depths. Two of our own group died during the arduous journey, one was Khacher's widow's sister. We were unable to bury them because we had neither shovel nor pickax. All we could do was cover their bodies with cloth, say a sad farewell to them, and leave them at the roadside.

In Intilli, after several rugged, depressing days of travel, we found and rented an empty store across from a Turkish baker named Mustafa and crowded ourselves into it. Papazian, happy to see Krikor and to help us, quickly assigned us to jobs. I was fortunate in being chosen to work under the surveyor, Mr. Fracello, an interpreter. We both knew French. He would convey instructions to me in that language and I would translate them for the workers.

Our group of families believed we now were safe and free from further deportations. But such dreams were to evaporate into thin air! In that spring of 1916, strict orders came by telegram that the fifty thousand Armenians working on the railway tunnels from Intilli and Aydun all the way to Aleppo had to be deported, immediately and without exception, to designated exile locations.

After having worked hardly a month and a half, we were to become part of a caravan to far-off Biridjik (now Birecik) on the banks of the Euphrates. Our route was to be by way of Fundujak, Marash, and Aintab. Those remaining alive would be sent to Rasiulia. There, we learned to our horror, Chechens were waiting like impatient hunters for the arrival of Armenian deportees.

Despite efforts by Mr. Fracello and a Swiss engineer, Mr. Keopelli, to have me remain, I, along with many others, was arrested. This happened without my family's knowledge because I was at work at the time. I asked to be allowed to go to my family and was told I would be with them in Baghche, that they already were on their way there. That much was true. I was taken to Baghche where about eighteen hundred persons were being assembled to form a caravan that would follow the same route as one that had left a few days before.

With a stranger's help, I was able to buy a donkey so that Beatrice, who had recovered much of her strength, and my mother-in-law could take turns riding as we traveled. I again would carry our child. We were permitted to take only our bedding and the child's clothing. We would be overseen, and supposedly protected, by forty policemen assigned by the head of the Baghche gendarmes, a monster named Yasher Bey.

—Trail of Horror—

Before our caravan left, known clergymen and teachers were removed from it and taken to a house which, we learned later, had been set on fire while they were trapped inside.

We started out toward evening. We had proceeded hardly two hours before we began coming upon the most atrocious scenes imaginable! Thrown alongside the roadway or in ravines were naked bodies from the caravan that had preceded us. They were older people or very small children who had been unable to keep up with the pace of the caravan. They had been stabbed to death and looted. By the time we reached the village of Dushburak, two of our group had suffered the same fate.

In Dushburak, ten lovely girls were whisked off by the policemen leading us. There was no doubt about what would happen to them. They were being taken to the local police station to be ravished by the police. Horrified, I feared for Beatrice. To camouflage her youth, I changed the appearance of her face by smudging it with soot and mud to make her look old. We were only beginning to experience the terrible things that were to take place before we would reach the bloody banks of the Euphrates on our way to the desert.

When we drew close to Fundujak, Turkish villagers attacked us and grabbed four girls to take away with them. How pathetic was the shrieking and crying of those girls as they struggled to free themselves! But how futile. The Turks also set upon two male youths. An Armenian woman tried to stop them. She and her child were brutally stabbed to death on the spot! All the while, our police escorts stood by smirking and smiling, fully enjoying what they saw.

Shortly after these episodes, policemen who had been escorting the first caravan appeared. They asked our police how the losses were going, obviously the more, the better. "A few," came the answer, almost apologetic in its tone. At that moment, there was gunfire, both in front of us and in back. Many innocent persons fell to the ground. The answer now could be considerably more than "a few."

Soon we were diverted to the bank of a stream for encampment and for our escorting police to rest. Chaos quickly followed. Another band of Turkish villagers, with no attempt by our police "protectors" to stop them, descended on us with hatchets, scythes, shovels, truncheons, and sickles. They slew nearly five hundred persons. Not content with that slaughter, they took with them as captives many of the younger men and women.

In these ways, almost fifty thousand Armenians would be annihilated in the Intilli and Fundujak regions. In the midst of these horrible events one grasped that the purpose of the Turkish government was to wipe out the Armenian presence in the Ottoman Empire.

—Our Dwindling Number—

The police escorting us stated that if we would give them money, they would protect the remaining caravan. Under the leadership of Khushagian of Marash, we collected five hundred gold Ottomans and handed them over to the police leader. We wanted to believe this extortion would put an end to the crimes against us. But this was a naive and false hope.

Not long after, a Turkish official from Marash appeared with eight gendarmes. They assembled all of us and looked us over carefully. Many judged to be young were herded into a separate group. Soon they were marched away, not to return. We had no way of knowing their fate, except that it would be harrowing whatever it was. As I watched the terror on the faces of the young women who were going, I was ever so thankful that I had smudged Beatrice's face to make her look old.

At another spot along the way, an unbelievably horrible thing happened. The police began a purge of infants crying from hunger and the other forms of terrible distress they were undergoing. With unbridled brutality, they were torn from the arms of their terrified mothers and thrown like bags of refuse into a large stream nearby. I trembled for little Koharig, but she was spared.

When one of our group, Kasab Setrak of Aintab, tried to protest this criminal treatment that knew no bounds, a dagger quickly pierced his heart. A man named Manoug from Hasan Beyli, who had worked with the chief engineer on the Intilli tunnel, also tried to speak out. He, too, fell to the ground just in front of me, blood spurting from a dagger wound that penetrated his chest. His wife and child could not bear the pain of watching his dead body being dragged aside and looted. His wife later said he had eight hundred Ottomans tied to his waist.

Thus far, my family and I had not been subjected to any type of assault. My turn came, however, when fatigue caused me to walk more slowly and I began dropping back. One of the policemen landed a powerful blow with the butt of his rifle on my back, also hitting little Koharig. She let out a piercing scream. The partner of the attacking policeman protested: "Say, man, he's got an innocent child on his back. Take pity on him." Thanks to my child's scream, we both were saved. I summoned all the strength I could and ran to the head of the group. After that I tried always to walk well up forward and not fall back. Many old persons and small children were being clubbed to death because they could not keep up with the pace.

One evening we stopped at the filthy sewer canal south of Marash to spend the night. All of us, extremely tired, slept under covers. The police watched to make sure we did not get up to find clean water. And during the night they began lifting covers to look for adult males. They took away those they selected, ostensibly to get watermelons from nearby fields. But those taken did not return. Several times I carefully crawled from one spot to another, choosing areas that already had been searched. It was a terrifying night!

We who were still there the next morning continued on like columns of ants toward Aintab. For days, we walked silently to the east along difficult and rocky paths. It is impossible to describe, and for anyone who wasn't there to visualize, the pain, the hunger, and exhaustion. The wonder is that any of us endured at all! Many mothers who still had their infants and were too weak to carry them any longer had to abandon them in mountain passes and along roadsides. The agony of seeing those helpless little humans left there to die was unbearable. But the only choice the mothers had was to lie down and die with them or trudge on.

With each hour, our pathetic band of tormented souls grew smaller. Many along the way just fell dead and were heaved aside by the police after being searched for anything of value that might be hidden in what was left of their clothing. To others, gasping from exhaustion and faltering behind, death came by bayonet. At points along the route, Turkish mobs swarmed on us like vultures, torturing and raping with complete freedom. The police, instead of offering protection, frequently entertained themselves by going after the women as if in a hunting game. Somehow, my mother-in-law was spared.

July was excessively hot. Mouths and throats were parched and raw for lack of water. Finally, after we had walked for what seemed an endless time, we came to a well in the village of Sinan near Aintab. Turks in charge of the well had to be paid for a cup of water. I gave up my coat to buy water for my family.

As we moved on, my mother-in-law, her will to live unbelievably strong, insisted that her daughter ride in the saddle on our donkey. She tried also not to fall behind the caravan, for the police were bayoneting stragglers. And I, with what seemed supernatural strength, kept going on the road to Golgotha with my child tied to my back.

Since we would be passing close to Aintab, I suggested to Ovsanna that she might want to try to escape into the city, her birthplace, and possibly find relatives or acquaintances with whom she could stay. But she declined, saying she did not want to part from us.

We continued on our way, over and between mountains, through villages, past green fields and orchards. At last we reached the village of Nizib, across from Biridjik and near the Euphrates River. This time the police allowed us to put our feet into a small stream and rest, mainly because they needed rest themselves. We quenched our thirst by drinking the water from the palms of our hands.

After the police had rested a while, they wanted to find out how many of us had survived. They counted the number by having us get to the other side of the stream one by one. Of the eighteen hundred who had left the tunnel area at Intilli, only four hundred had reached Nizib!

After we crossed the stream, our donkey fell to the ground completely exhausted. It was almost as if the poor animal wanted to tell us he had fulfilled his duty during those frightful days. It was impossible to get him to his feet. We had nearly reached the Euphrates. There was nothing we could do but leave the faithful animal there to his own fate. So we continued on downhill. After walking a total of fifteen days, we were on the sandy banks of the Euphrates opposite Biridjik. There we joined a crowded mass of more than fifty thousand deportees from various places. All, like us, were hungry, half naked, and barefoot. It was hard to look at the faces of many because they were so contorted and gnarled.

—Escape or Perish—

Deportees from far-off Marzifan and Malatya related the intense suffering they had endured in traveling over mountains and through valleys in their long trek to Biridjik. They told of the trials of their young, their old, the mothers carrying delicate infants. They recounted the covering of corpses of those who had fallen victim to pitiless torture by the policemen who constantly plagued them. Thousands had been thrown off mountain peaks or committed to the rushing waters of the Euphrates and Tigris. Countless others had been stabbed and left to die agonizing deaths. And many others had taken their own lives to hold high and preserve Armenian honor by their deaths.

In truth, the Turks were committing genocide of a kind unknown throughout human history. Yet, no cry of anger and protest was raised by Christian nations against this infamous crime that filled one of the blackest chapters in the long story of mankind.

On top of the carnage inflicted by the Turks, an epidemic of typhus struck us while we were being held on the banks of the Euphrates. Each day hundreds were dying from it. My dear wife Beatrice fell ill from the terrible disease. Her mother and I were totally distraught by her suffering and the grave danger of losing her.

Turkish women kept coming from nearby villages to sell madzoun (yogurt), milk, tun (yogurt mixed with water), and other products from their farms. I was able to buy from one of them a container for fluid made of goat hide. This enabled me to carry water from the Euphrates to Beatrice. The water helped, but I knew I must do more.

There was an old, abandoned khan (inn) nearby. I went up the very narrow steps to its roof and fashioned the best tent I could with the only cover we still had. This served to provide shade for my sick wife, my mother-in-law, and little Koharig. Men helped me carry Beatrice to the roof, and we laid her gently in the shade. But her condition worsened! She reached a point at which she hardly could breathe!

Fortunately, I had been able to keep my razor. I used it to make a few cuts in her forehead so that some blood would flow out. My mother-in-law disapproved. "My son," she pleaded, "don't torture my daughter for nothing. She is already dead." But I was determined. "Mother, I will not let her die," I answered firmly. After making the cuts with the razor, I poured water on Beatrice's head, then gently rubbed her forehead, her cheeks and her neck. Soon she opened her eyes, looked up at me, and took a deep breath. What a moment it was! "See, mother," I said joyfully. "Your daughter did not die. She is going to live!"

Hundreds in front of the khan and on the banks of the river continued to die daily. Geoz Demirji Sarkis, one of our relatives from Baghche, suddenly turned black and died right before our eyes. In order to protect Beatrice from seeing these horrible scenes, we moved her to an empty corner inside the khan and settled down there. We not only were less visible to the police, but were spared the unbearable sights outside. We could not avoid sorrow inside, however. Settled in another corner of the khan was the family of Jindar Vanes, of Baghche. All lying sick with the black typhus, the whole family died before our eyes!

Meanwhile, a few hundred deportees each day were being carried across the river in large barges. From there, they would be driven on to slaughterhouses where two-legged beasts, including criminals set free from prisons, were ready to revel in the blood they savagely would draw.

According to the rumors constantly flying around, all of us eventually would come to the same end. An inseparable friend, Ohan Karoghlanian, and I knew that somehow we had to escape before our turn came. West of the Euphrates from Biridjik was a village whose leader was a farsighted, considerate Turk named Kadir Effendi. He had taken many deportees to the village and placed them there as artisans and farm workers. We learned that among them were some of our relatives from Baghche. At the same time, we heard that Kadir Effendi's brother, Asaf Effendi, also was looking for workers.

We were able to get a message through to the brother. Six families of us applied to him as farmworkers. While we were waiting to hear back, hoping our turns would not come up to be taken across the river, a Turkish woman from the Biridjik village of Yokare Bayundur came to sell milk, yogurt, and tun. She told me she was looking for a woman to take back to the village as a companion for her. She said she was alone and was sad because her only son had been taken into the army and she had received no word from him. She wanted someone with whom she could spend time and find solace.

When I told my mother-in-law about this, she agreed to go to the village with the woman. Beatrice had nearly recovered and could take care of our child without her mother's help. Ovsanna thought that by going to

My mother-in-law, Ovsanna Panosian.

the village, she would find a way for us to go there as well. With that hope, she left. We could not imagine it would be the last time we would see her.

Our situation was desperate! The barges constantly were crossing the river with their loads of doomed deportees. Any of us still waiting were in imminent danger of being herded onto those carriers to death. It was imperative that we do something quickly.

We devised and followed a plan. The husbands in our small group of families succeeded in stealing out during the night to a nearby cemetery. Evading dozing policemen, our families miraculously managed to join us. Then we left, a silent band of nomads watching every anxious instant for any sign or sight of the dreaded police.

It was a plan that worked! We escaped to Asaf Effendi's village.

— No Relief from Danger —

Although it turned out that Asaf Effendi did not need workers, he let us camp in a large courtyard next to his house. The inhabitants of the village were mostly Kurds, and there were a few Turks. All were friendly and wanted to help us as much as they could. The wheat they had planted had been harvested, however, leaving us no means of earning a living. All we could do was go into the fields and gather up what wheat still lay there. We took this to a nearby village and had it milled into flour. In addition, we were glad to perform even the lowliest of tasks wherever we could find them.

We had been there hardly a month and a half when we heard that the police were rounding up deportees hiding in the villages and sending them to Deir ez Zor, which, along with Rasiulia, had become notorious as a major center for the annihilation of Armenians. In an effort to avoid being taken, we collected whatever money we could from among us. It amounted to ten gold Ottomans, a sum we turned over to Asaf Effendi to give to the police as ransom to spare us.

At the same time, tragedy struck for Beatrice and me. As was true with all of us, our little daughter Koharig was emaciated from lack of food. It was impossible to look at her tiny, pathetic body without being overcome by sadness and anger.

Koharig's custom was to sleep at night with her head on my arm. This particular night, what only could be considered a supernatural phenomenon, occurred! At exactly midnight, an arc-shaped light appeared suddenly. Like a rainbow, it reached down to her. Bewildered, I began to pray. In a short time, the light disappeared. And at that moment, our little one stopped breathing. Her sinless soul surely had soared with the light of that rainbow. Shaken, I took some comfort in knowing she no longer would have to endure the pain and suffering our terrible plight had inflicted on her innocent body.

To delay Beatrice's anguish, I did not waken her until morning. Then everyone knew what had happened. I went immediately to neighboring Kurds and asked them for a pick and shovel so that I might bury the little body in a suitable spot on a nearby hillside. There it would not be disturbed. When finished, I prayed over the mound and, in tears, left it.

Three days later, villagers informed us that the police were coming to get all of us. We men, eight in number, were advised to go away and hide in the mill to which we had taken the wheat gathered up from the fields. We left at once for the village where it was located, hoping the women and children would not be taken without us.

We soon learned that when the police arrived at Asaf Effendi's village, they demanded to be told where we were. A girl from Hasan Beyli, whose fiancé was with us, innocently divulged our hiding place. The police leader grabbed the girl, took her on his horse, and, followed by other police, came to the mill. They began to interrogate us. Then, after forcing us to remove our clothes, they started to beat and rob us, taking everything they could find.

They found a paper in my pocket, gloating that it was a treacherous letter. "That is not a letter!" I exclaimed. "Read it. It is a list showing that ten gold Ottomans were collected among us and turned over to the agha who was to give them to you." None of the policemen could read or write. I read to them the names I had written in Turkish of those who had given the money.

The police were surprised and pleased to get this information. The leader instructed the others to take us back to Asaf Effendi's village, collect the money, then take us to Biridjik to be judged before a military court. He spurred his horse, and with the girl, rode off toward Nizib.

When we got back to the village, we found that our families had been forced to go to Meskene where deportees from other villages also had been taken. After scorning Asaf Effendi and collecting the ten Ottomans, the police ordered that a good quantity of pilaf be prepared to feed themselves and us.

Artisan relatives of ours who had been brought to Kadir Effendi's village from Baghche had seen our families being taken away and knew the men were not among them. The

main road to Biridjik on which the police took us happened to pass directly in front of Kadir Effendi's house.
On seeing us approach, the relatives pleaded with him to
save me, saying I could be helpful to him, that I knew
many languages, and that I could teach his children
Turkish. Kadir Effendi came out to the road and shouted
to the police to halt. "Who among you is Mugrditch
Oghlan (son of Mugrditch)?" he asked. I immediately
answered. He took hold of my arm and said, This giavour
(non-Moslem) is useful to us." The police responded,
"Your servant, Effendi."

Thus I was left with him. I was sorry the other members of our group of men couldn't be spared with me and
only could hope that they, too, would escape in some way.

Kadir Effendi enjoyed a high level of esteem among
Turkish government officials. I was sure that for the time
being at least I would be safe. And I was overjoyed that
evening when my close friend Ohan Karoghanian came
and joined me. He had been at work in another village
and the police had not found him. His family, however,
had been taken to Meskene along with the others.

After remaining in Kadir Effendi's village for two days,
Ohan and I decided that we must get to Meskene and find
our families. Through everything that had happened I had
managed to keep my wedding ring hidden. But now I had
no choice but to sell it in order to get money that would
be needed for the journey. Once this was done, I asked
Kadir Effendi for permission to go with Ohan to Meskene
to find my wife and for someone who knew the way to
accompany us. I firmly promised that if I remained alive,
I surely would return.

"Are you crazy?" Kadir Effendi exploded. "Having a
wife here would be too much for you!" But I finally per-

suaded him, and he assigned us an Anouze Arab for hire. Wearing turbans on our heads and mantles on our backs, Ohan and I took off with the guide.

After walking for five days, we reached an Arab village near the fortress of Membidj (now Manbij). The Anouze Arab wanted more money to take us on to Meskene, nine hours away. "Take us there first," we said. "Then we'll give you the money you want. Our families have money. We have no more." He refused and left us.

We stopped at the house of a friendly Arab. He gave us some grapes and watermelon. Also he offered us encouragement by saying, "After dark, I will take you to Membidj. There is a khan there where muleteers who go to Meskene often stay. You can go to Meskene with them." And that night he took us to the city.

—A Happy Surprise—

When we knocked on the door of the khan, a youth opened it. After peering straight into my eyes a moment, he embraced me and cried out, "Haji Effendi!" Then he led us in.

It was an amazing, and for us, most fortunate, turn of events! I once had placed that youth—his name was Boghos—in the Kelegian-Sisouan Orphanage at Deortyol. He took us to his room; the owner of the inn had made him the manager. We talked and recalled past events until morning.

We told Boghos of our plans, but he warned us against going to Meskene. "As soon as you get there, they will arrest you and send you to Deir ez Zor," he said. "An Armenian artisan family and three other Armenians are in

a village close to here. One of them, Atesh Oghlou, is looking for additional workers to build two more rooms to his
house. You can work there safely and we'll think about
what to do regarding your families." His warning changed
our minds about going to Meskene; we had to face reality.

The next day Atesh Oghlou, having been told by Boghos
that we would be fine workers, came to the khan to take
Ohan and me to his village. Before leaving, I quickly wrote
a note to Beatrice. Boghos knew the guard at the refugee station in Meskene—the man was from Sis—and was sure the
note, taken to him by muleteers, would get to my wife. I told
her where Ohan and I were, asked her to write back to me,
and said we would try to rescue her.

Not long after, a return letter came from her. She told
us not to try to come to Meskene because it was extremely dangerous. But at least we had established a means of
communication.

In Atesh Oghlou's village, we went to work on the two
rooms he was adding to his house. In this we joined three
other men, one an expert mason. For the construction,
which was a lengthy process, we first had to cast and fash-
ion adobe blocks, then dry them in the sun.

Atesh Oghlou gave Ohan and me some bread each day
and sometimes dry pilaf, but the amounts never were
enough to keep us from being hungry. At night, in order
to stay out of the cold, we slept in the barn where the animals were kept. The days were warm, but quickly turned
cold after dark, and we had meager clothing. Our duties
also included bringing water from a well for all the needs
of the house and the animals. And we gathered thistle
from the fields for fuel.

As if we didn't have enough problems, we were beset by
an infestation of lice. What little clothing we needed had

to be washed constantly. One day I put out my just-washed shirt to dry on the grass. A cow from the grazing herd bit into the arm of the garment and carried it away. I was able to retrieve the shirt, but one sleeve was missing. So I had a one-armed shirt to go with what were badly-patched pants.

Two girls from among the deportees were at Atesh Ouglou's house. When the master was asleep, they sometimes would bring us bread and other leftover food, even a handful of wheat. How grateful we were for their kindness.

Another girl in the village suffered a terrible fate! Armenian and only thirteen years old, she had been seized from a caravan by Salih, son-in-law of the village chief. One day, half-starved, she stole an egg and was eating it. Salih, a monster, punished her by throwing her into a forty-meter-deep dry well. Inhumanity knows no limits!

—*Unwavering Faith*—

At night the Arabs would gather under a tent in the center of the village and sing a monotonous song to the accompaniment of a two-string tamboura. Sometimes we would go there and watch. There was a boy, thirteen or fourteen years old, who also would come. One evening, looking into his eyes, I asked, "Are you Armenian?" His answer was a firm, "No. I'm an Arab." We learned that he was a shepherd for one of the wealthy families of the village. Later, he confessed to me that he was Armenian. We gradually became friendly. I tried to inspire in him the faith that one day we would be liberated from our oppression. When I found out two years later that he had escaped to Aleppo and freedom, I was gratified for having given him that hope.

My own physical condition became a problem. An inflammation developed in my right jaw and in my ear. The pain was so intense that I was unable to speak. In this miserable state, many thoughts and recollections paraded through my mind.

I recalled my mother, hardly twenty-six years old when she was widowed. Her tenacious hope and indomitable will enabled her to rear and nurture four children. And my two brothers, who were martyred, were brave to the end. I thought of our innocent child, little Koharig and my dear wife Beatrice.

These thoughts and memories filled me with courage and reinforced my will to survive. My hopes would rise even at the most dreadful times. I resolved that I would not lose faith under any circumstances and that I would live.

One evening when we were seated in the yard talking, one of our group, Rouben from Deortyol, became demented. He started to jump around crazily. Dismayed, I lifted my eyes toward heaven and prayed for help from God. Suddenly I saw a shooting star, wonderfully bright and moving swiftly. It took on the shape of a letter as it sped across the sky—the letter h. I called out to my companions, "Look, boys! In the sky! There is the letter h. That stands for hye (Armenian). It is a symbol that Armenians will live and be free. Believe it. Have faith, never give up hope."

We had to believe in miracles, and the vision of the shooting star was indeed a miracle. It has been said: "If it had hailed that much, the stones would have been beaten to dust." Hard as the hail of oppression, torture, and near annihilation pounded us, the fire of hope within us, the strength of our inner faith, and our will would lead us again to survive as a people.

Soon after that miracle, a Kurdish woman living near us noticed my poor physical condition. She offered to cure me, saying she wanted to help an Armenian in return for the good treatment Armenians had given her soldier son when he fell prisoner in Van. I gladly accepted her offer.

This grateful woman gathered some grasses from the field and cooked them with flour to make a hot poultice, which she tied to my jaw. She repeated this process several times. In a few days the swollen area opened and discharged its pus. The pain subsided and before long my condition was entirely cured. The woman fulfilled her wish to help an Armenian; my appreciation was unbounded.

It took close to six months to finish adding the two rooms to Atesh Oghlou's house. Ohan and I were free to stay either in the village or in the city of Membidj. And I thought about my promise to Kadir Effendi that if I remained alive, I would return. I was sorry to go back on that promise, but it was best to be closer to Meskene in the hope that a way still would be found to rescue my wife and Ohan's family.

A letter from Beatrice arrived shortly after. It had been some time since I had heard from her and I was greatly concerned about her. Now there was wonderful news! She had escaped from Meskene and was working with her aunt (her father's sister) at the Imaret Khan in Aleppo, and was living with her aunt. She suggested that I try to join her. The thought of being with her again filled me with determination to get to Aleppo, whatever the danger I might undergo in doing so. Ohan was happy for me and urged me to go. We only wished he had received similar news about his family.

73

–VI–

Reunion in Aleppo

In those days groups of Kurdish traders from Edessa and Mosul passed through Membidj on their way to the Bab region of Aleppo to buy salt to take back and sell. On their journeys they stopped overnight at the khan Boghos managed. It so happened that Boghos had a long-standing friendship with one of the chiefs of those traders. He was confident his friend would get me safely to Aleppo.

In anticipation of this, I gathered together ragged clothing thrown into trash heaps. Sewing them together into a long band, I made a kiulah (turban). Also I altered somewhat my one-sleeved shirt. And I fashioned a wooden staff to carry. Thus, for the trip, I would assume the appearance of a Kurd.

Not long afterward the chief arrived at the khan with his group of Kurds and their donkeys. Boghos conferred with him before introducing me. The chief carefully looked me over then nodded his head and agreed to take me. I was relieved and delighted.

The chief advised me never to speak while we traveled. He said that if I were asked whether I understood

Kurdish, I only should answer with the word chizani ("I don't understand"). In other words, for my own protection, I was to remain silent. I did just that.

After traveling for five days, we arrived in Bab. Faithful to his agreement, the chief took me to a hotel in Aleppo, then returned to Bab to rejoin the other Kurds. He and Boghos are high among the many individuals to whom, for their help during that terrible period of travail, I have owed a lifetime of gratitude.

At the hotel, I rested a while and dried my shirt, wet from a downpour that had struck us. My recollection was that a friend, the teacher Ovsanna of Kharne, was in the Azizia parish of Aleppo. I would go to her first.

With the kiulah on my head and the staff on my shoulder, I went to the parish house. I knocked on the courtyard door. God was with me. It was Ovsanna herself who opened the door a crack and peered at this masquerading Kurd. She recognized me at once and gleefully wrapped her arms around my neck. We went directly to her room.

Ovsanna and I knew each other well. She was at my wedding. We had kept in close contact when she was a teacher in the Armenian school of Kharne and I was a teacher in Lapajle in 1913. After exchanging information on our various experiences and filling my starved stomach, she led me to the Imaret Khan. On her advice, I followed five to ten meters behind. When we reached the khan and knocked on the door, Mrs. Manoushagian, director of the tailoring section there, answered. After we explained why we had come, she called Beatrice's aunt Rahel to the door. Rahel greeted me warmly, and in tears, called Beatrice.

After eight months, we were together again. Mrs. Manoushagian led us to the rooftop where we could be alone and experience the wondrous joy of being together after so long a time.

Naturally I was anxious to hear what had happened to Beatrice during those anxious eight months. The following is her own recounting of what she had experienced.

—*Beatrice's Story*—

When the police came to Asaf Effendi's village and the girl from Hasan Beyli inadvertently told them where the men were hiding, the leader ordered some of his squad to march the women and children to Meskene. With the girl on his horse and the rest of the members of his squad behind him, he took off to find the men.

We were hungry, barefoot, and had to walk under indescribable conditions. Those who could not keep up were killed with daggers. Many young persons were taken away by Arabs to become their servants. After seven days of walking and unbelievable suffering, we were very much decimated when we reached Meskene.

At Meskene, there were about one hundred thousand Armenians spread out on the banks of the Euphrates. They were in a most wretched condition, waiting for their turns to be driven to Ragga or Deir ez Zor, the last way stations of their death march. Large numbers were dying daily from starvation and sickness.

Observing these heart-rending scenes, despairing that my husband had been shot to death, and believing that none of my family or relatives were left, I decided that I would not fall into the hands of the Turks or the claws of the Arabs. I would end my life with honor. So I made the sign of the cross and threw myself into the Euphrates River.

An acquaintance, a girl from Sis, saw this. She shouted for help. I was pulled from the river, unconscious. When I opened my eyes, I found myself in a tent with strangers except for the girl from Sis. Her sister, who later died, had been a classmate of mine at school in Sis. The tent belonged to her parents. When she told them her sister and I had been friends, her father, Santour agha Bekmezjian, said I would stay with them in the tent.

So I lived on, in tears, with none of us knowing when our time would come to die. I spent the days gathering camel droppings and selling them to those who had money. The droppings were used for fuel; there was nothing else to be found in the desert that would provide fuel for needed fires.

One day Santour agha brought me a letter and made me promise not to cry when I read it; the people were tired of seeing me crying all the time. The letter was from my husband. He was alive! He had found refuge in Membidj and was trying to find means of coming to Meskene to join me. When I read the letter to Santour agha, he said, "Your husband must not leave where he is. No one knows what will happen to us here. Since he is safe where he is, let him stay there. If he comes to Meskene, he immediately will be sent to Deir ez Zor and death."

So I wrote to Hovhannes and told him not to put his life in danger, but to wait for better days. The letter was sent to him by the same muleteers who had brought his to me.

Several days later, Santour agha, in a state of high agitation, huddled us together in the tent. "I heard they are going to clear out Meskene," he said. "All of us are to be

sent to Deir ez Zor, our final grave. We have to escape!"
He explained that their daughter and two sons, along with
Ohan Karoghlanian's wife and me, must creep out that
very night and head for Aleppo. He and his wife would
see what they could do later.

That night the five of us crawled from the tent and into
fields of thistles. The sharp prickles were painful as they
kept piercing our skin, but our only choice was to endure
the pain in order to get away. Soon we changed from
crawling to walking, silent and watchful every instant.
When dawn came, we hid in bushes and stayed there until
night. This we did each successive day as we made slow,
difficult progress toward Aleppo. But that progress was to
be interrupted!

We were in a ravine, quenching our thirst by a stream,
when we found ourselves suddenly surrounded by Arabs.
They pounced on us. Each of us was grabbed by one of
them and taken away, some on horseback, some walking.
My captor was on foot, and he wrapped my hair twice
around his wrist so I could not escape.

After walking some distance in agony from my hair constantly being pulled, a man on horseback approached. He
spoke with my captor in Arabic. I understood enough of
it to know what was being said. The Arab insisted he was
not going to kill me, but was going to make me his wife.
The horseman asked me to look up. I did so and said in
Armenian, "I am the wife of the teacher in Osmaniye."

"So I was not wrong," the horseman said. He had recognized me, and spoke to the Arab again in Arabic. "Her
husband is a captain in the city of Sham," he said. "I will
wire him. He will come and kill you and take back his
wife." On hearing that, the Arab let go of my hair,
wrapped his arms around the horseman's leg, and cried

out, "Have pity!" Then he ran off.

In that way I was saved. My rescuer took me up on his horse. As we left, he explained that he was an Assyrian and that one evening he had been a guest at our house and had eaten a michov keufta (keufta with filling). He told me he owned a khan down the way.

He asked where I had been captured by the Arab. I told him what had happened, but I didn't know just where the stream from which we had been drinking was located. He had no trouble finding it, however. And Santour's older boy was there crying. The Arab who grabbed him had changed his mind and set him free.

The Assyrian took us to his khan and put us in the stable. Then he left to search for the others who had been taken by the Arabs. By evening, after hours of looking, he found Santour's younger boy, who was nine years old. He was unable to locate the others. He brought us some food and warned us not to make any sound during the night.

Two nuns arrived by cart from Deir ez Zor and were staying at the khan. They were to leave for Aleppo early in the morning. A policeman was with them driving the cart. The Assyrian bribed him to let us accompany the nuns and to protect us as we passed two Arab villages. I expressed my deep thanks to my rescuer and told him I hoped he, my husband, and I would meet again under happier circumstances.

The policeman drove the cart slowly so the boys and I could walk along with it. We had no trouble until we were close to Aleppo. The cart began moving more swiftly and we could not keep up with it. Santour's sons and I soon became separated from one another in the suburbs of the city. I was in near panic! As I looked around, confused and not knowing what to do, four or five Aleppo children called out, "Some refugees are coming from Meskene." At that moment, a woman came up to me and told me to follow her. I walked along behind her.

The woman went to a house and asked me to come inside. Her son, who had been wounded in the military service, was there. She walked to the back of the house and returned with an uzar (robe) worn outdoors by Arabs. She dressed me in it. Then she directed her son, who had a donkey, to lead me to the Imaret Khan. But she wanted money. I had only a quarter mejide (coin) with me. She was satisfied with that. So, following the son at some distance, we arrived at the Imaret Khan military workshops. I gave him his mother's robe and the quarter mejide, and he left.

Upon entering the building, I found that all the workers there were Armenians. They asked me what village I had come from and I told them I was from Aintab. They called the manager who also was a native of Aintab. After much inquiry about my family connections, he said, "Your father's sister is here, working as a designer in the tailoring section." They called my Aunt Rahel. What a welcome sight she was! With tears of joy, we embraced. In a while, they pinned on me a passage permit badge belonging to someone else, and my aunt took me home to her house. I would receive my own permit in two days; it was necessary to have one in order to work at the khan. And I was assured I would have a job there.

Before going to work, I had to have medical attention. My feet were covered with sores, and painful thorns embedded in my feet, legs and arms had to be removed. Other parts of my body had been cut and bruised also during the long, grueling walk from Meskene to Aleppo.

When these conditions had been treated, I went to work with my aunt in the tailoring section of the khan. For wages, I received three meals a day. Soon I was able to move freely in the city because I was an employee at the Imaret Khan. It was then that I wrote Hovhannes and asked him to try to escape to Aleppo. What a joyful day it was when he arrived toward the end of March, 1917.

—Life Renewed—

With Beatrice safe and secure in working at the Imaret Khan, I was determined to find something that would enable me to remain in Aleppo with her. Rahel and her husband Arakel, a barber, were kind in letting me stay at their house while I looked for a job. But I soon learned I was not out of danger!

When Arakel was cutting my hair and shaving me in

Beatrice's Aunt Rahel and Uncle Arakel in 1925.

the courtyard of his house, two policemen burst suddenly into the yard. They said they were going to arrest me and exile me to Deir ez Zor. Arakel cleverly admonished them, "Shame on you for wanting to arrest a man in a half-shaved condition! Let me finish my work. Then I'll send him to the police station." The policemen, being acquainted with Arakel and having received free haircuts from him, left. And I, not waiting for Arakel to finish his work, took to the rooftops, scurrying from one to another until I reached the house of Beatrice's relative, Haroutiun, and took refuge there. Haroutiun, whom I had visited a short time before, was a servant in the household of the governor of Aleppo.

Even though I did not know how to use a hammer and saw adroitly, I was obliged to apply to the Imaret Khan as a carpenter. Fortunately, I didn't have to display my ineptness with those tools of the trade. Instead, my job was to carry such tools for master carpenters from Deortyol. My wages, the same as Beatrice's, were three meals a day. But the main thing was that being employed at the khan gave me at least some measure of safety from deportation.

Sometime later, I became acquainted with a man known as kind-hearted Jack from Constantinople. He was an interpreter at one of the German military hospitals. On learning my history and background, he took an interest in me and suggested that, to assure my safety, I go to work at the hospital. He took me there, and immediately I was given a job as a cook's helper. And of paramount importance, I obtained a document signed by a German colonel, exempting me from exile to Deir ez Zor.

As helper to two cooks, I began my work. My pay was two gold Ottomans a month. I worked hard and it didn't take long to win praise from the hospital officials. The

German cooks, Schneider and Bilen, were drinkers. They also sold some of the foodstuffs, such as tins of cooking oils, to other hospitals. After a time, nearly all details were left to me. I began to study German so I could communicate better with the cooks. And I rented a room where Beatrice and I could live alone. At the same time, I took her out of the Imaret Khan so she could rest. She was very tired, still worn out from the ordeals she had suffered.

The Germans had five military hospitals in Aleppo and surroundings. Because so many workers in the hospitals often were lazy and unreliable, I was called on, through Jack the interpreter, to find trustworthy Armenians for jobs there. At first they wanted five persons to deliver foodstuffs and to perform other miscellaneous duties. I went to the Armenian church and talked with the kahana. Through him, I found five individuals for whom I was able to secure work permits so they would not be arrested. I pressed them to behave in such a way that they would hold the Armenian name high. This was for the sake of their own and others' security and freedom.

Later, Jack asked me to find six women to do laundry and cleaning. I went immediately to Beatrice's Aunt Rahel, and through her, found five women and herself. She considered it preferable to work with the Germans than at the Imaret Khan. I also brought her husband, Arakel, to be barber for the soldiers, as well as his fifteen-year-old son, Gaspar, to deliver hospital meals. And in due course, I was able to enlist others.

Soon I was being asked by other German hospitals to find workers for them. They called me Houlianos (Julian) because the Germans had a hard time saying Hovhannes. They wanted reliable workers, and I was able to satisfy their needs pretty well. My recollection is that I placed forty-eight persons in those military hospitals.

The one at which I worked had a rectangular opening in the north wall near the kitchen. Leftover food was thrown through that opening to a hole in the ground just outside. There were many hungry and naked orphans on the streets and in the churchyard. An idea occurred to me. Why not give them the leftover food that was being thrown out?

Before going to their rooms at night, the two German cooks would give me instructions about cleaning the kitchen, getting rid of the leftovers, and performing other tasks. So there was an opportunity for me to do the humanitarian thing. I knew a few of the orphans and spoke with one of them, Sarkis Haygaroun Aprahamian, telling him to have the group gather at the hole at a specified time and wait silently in line.

The procedure I followed was to pour water through the opening to wash and clean it. They came one by one to the opening. From the inside of the wall I would pass food to them, filling the tins and pails they had brought along.

This giving of leftover hospital food earned me the name "Father of orphans, father of the poor."

Schneider, the head cook, knew what I was doing. He approved of it, in fact. He told me that sometime earlier he had been in the Mosul area and had seen the suffering of the Armenian exiles. He also told me this: "Kemal Pasha, who was commander there at the time, would spend every evening with his high-level officers, amusing themselves by violating the pretty Armenian girls. In many places they had opened brothels for Turks, with Armenian girls and women forced to be available to Turkish soldiers free of charge." That was the nature of Mustafa Kemal, the man called Ataturk ("the father of the Turks"). This was the man who became Turkey's first president after it became a republic on October 29, 1923.

—Crumbling Fronts—

In early October 1918, rumors began circulating in Aleppo that the Turks at the Palestine front were retreating. In fact, during the nights of September 18-19, Armenian volunteers had taken the "impregnable" heights of Arara and broken the Turkish front.

An interesting story came with the news of the victory. A Turkish colonel had been taken prisoner. When he saw a soldier in a French uniform speaking Turkish, he asked, "Where did you learn Turkish?" The soldier answered, "We are Armenians, members of the Armenian volunteer legion." The colonel was surprised. "Are there still some Armenians left in the world?" he asked. The soldier pointed to the army of Armenian volunteers not far in the distance as proof that there indeed were Armenians very much alive. "Good for you!" the colonel exclaimed. "The Armenian nation will never die."

With such news, turmoil began to develop among the German officers at our hospital. The superintendent called me to his office and told me that they were going to get out of Aleppo. They would leave behind only the critically sick soldiers, sixty-three in number. "We believe in your trustworthiness, as we do with interpreter Jack," he said. "We are leaving the sick ones in your care. A nun will be helping you. Take good care of the patients until the British army enters Aleppo. Then you can hand over the hospital to the British. Boil three hundred eggs tonight for us who are leaving so we'll have something to eat along the way."

A few days after the officers left, we heard that some Arabs were planning to seize the hospital. To protect the lives of the sick, I organized our workers for defense. When we saw the Arabs coming, we stood on the balcony shouting, "Don't come near the hospital. You will be blown up by bombs!" The Arabs stopped short, then turned and left.

On October 25, 1918, the British army occupied Aleppo, and I turned over the sixty-three hospital patients to their care. On October 30 the defeat of the Turks and the cessation of hostilities were announced. There were no bounds to the joy and jubilation of those Armenians who had evaded Gehenna.

—*Torments Revisited*—

People in Aleppo filled the churches, grounds, and streets, making new acquaintances, telling about sufferings they had endured during the four years of horror, and describing events they had experienced or witnessed.

People of Kharput and Arapkir told how the Turks, to appease their savagery, had exhumed bodies of Armenian clergymen from the graves and put them on display. Among them were the remains of the patriarch of Agn, Der Hovhannes Tertzagian. Another was the body of the primate of Mush, Bishop Kharakhanian (my teacher of theology at the seminary in Jerusalem in 1904–1908). The fresh graves of other churchmen had been opened, their anointed bodies taken by mobs and dragged through the streets with ropes tied to their feet, then thrown into the nearby waters.

The Kharput and Arapkir people went on to tell how Vartan Vartabad, who succeeded Kharakhanian as primate of Mush, was invited along with the City Assembly and Parish Council to attend an important "consultative" meeting. They went to the government building at the appointed time. There they were doused with gasoline and set afire, lay and clergy alike. Others in the population were subjected to all sorts of torture: searing the soles of feet, tearing off fingernails, driving wooden pegs under the nails, lacerating gums, ripping the breastbone, paddling the feet, hanging newborn infants by the feet, and more.

A woman from Yozgad related that the primate of Yozgad, Bishop Nerses Danielian, and forty-two thousand Armenians savagely were killed there. When Turkish Talaat Pasha came through Yozgad, he ordered the corpses to be thrown into a deep pit and covered over so that no evidence of the killing would remain.

A resident of Pazmashen had this story: In order to mislead the Armenian people, a German Protestant minister, Ehmann, came to the village, Gospel in hand, and preached, "'Render to Caesar the things that are Caesar's, and to God the things that are God's.' I swear by the Gospel I hold in my hand that no harm will befall you if you give up all your weapons." But the truth was that the Germans were waiting for the exile and massacre of Armenians so that the copper in our churches and monasteries could be confiscated and used for fashioning cannons.

These varied stories were but illustrations of the blasphemy, treachery, and horror that marked those terrible years.

We learned in January 1919 that the Armenian volunteer legions had taken Cilicia and that, under an agreement between the British and the French, the territory had been turned over to the latter. Colonel Bremond, a Frenchman, had been named governor. This meant that those of us who miraculously had lived through the hell of deportation, fire, and sword—seared remnants of the Armenian people—could return to our homeland.

The trains leaving Aleppo had many of the wolves, including Armenian traitors, who had spilled Armenian blood. They were escaping to Konya and Constantinople by way of Adana. But Armenian legions were on the job. They were raiding the railway cars, liberating Armenian girls, and apprehending Armenian Vasaks (named after the traitorous prefect of Armenia during the Vartanants wars in the midfifth century) to be brought in and put to death. The traitor named Garabed, who was from Zeitun and was active at the time we were in Adana, was among them.

–VII–

No Peace for Us

On *February 25, 1919*, we returned to the city from which we had been deported, Osmaniye. All told, there were some one hundred twenty-five thousand people who survived to come back to Cilicia. But an idea of the terrible toll that had been wrought can be gained from the fact that only fifteen hundred of the ten thousand Armenians who had lived in Zeitun were still alive.

Those of us who survived were enthusiastic about the future. We were certain that the Allies would treat us well and that before long we would have our independence. So, full of spirit and faith, we began to rebuild our communities.

Beatrice and I were happy to find my mother's sister, midwife Mariam, still living. She had taken refuge with a miller. Also our dear Dr. Vahan Vanlian had survived; for a time, he had changed his name to Dr. Ziay. And we were able to locate a few friends who had escaped death. To take care of the religious needs of the returnees, His Holiness, Catholicos Sahag, sent Der Hovhannes Kahana Giuherian.

There was a sad note, though. We were grieved to find out that three days after we had left Aleppo, there was a massacre in the Jiuma marketplace of exiled Armenians. This had occurred under the very eyes of the powerful, "protective" British. This blow was extremely disturbing, but we could not let it deter us in going ahead with the work that lay before us.

Colonel Bremond, as commander in Cilicia, issued a decree requiring that all Armenian children and women under Turkish control were to be released in care of military officials. Turks who failed to comply would be subject to severe punishment and penalties.

Encouraged by this decree, I immediately set to work. My first step was to form an Armenian National Committee, of which, because I was acquainted with the local circumstances and knew the people, I served as secretary. We also organized a branch of the Armenian General Benevolent Union and collected four gold Ottomans as initial support money for it. This money was placed in the care of wealthy and trustworthy Roum Haji Agha. We were filled with enthusiasm and confidence, not thinking that again our people would undergo mass terror because the French would do nothing to stop it.

With the help of an interpreter, Hrant Baloian, I began looking for orphan boys and girls left with Turks, relying on him in matters calling for interaction with government officials. I had enjoyed a good relationship with local Turks; they always called me Haji Hoja (teacher who has been to Jerusalem). Because of my favorable standing with them, many came and told me where Armenian children were being kept. I also learned from them that my father's sister's grandchildren, left in the village of Karagedik at the time of the deportations, had died in the searing desert.

Through Hrant Baloian I asked for and was assigned three policemen to assist in gathering up orphans. One of the three was the brave gendarme Hovhannes of Zeitun with whom I already was acquainted. He had apprehended and killed the criminal who had subjected me to terror and robbed me in Osmaniye.

The first orphans the policemen brought me were a brother and sister to whom the names Osman and Fatima were given. My aunt Mariam revealed that Osman's name really was Sarkis and Fatima's was Mariam. But they had become Turkefied. While staying at our house for a week under the care of Beatrice, Sarkis tried several times to leave. "Fatima and I want our mother," he would say in Turkish. I had to send him along with eight other orphans to the Benevolent Union orphanage in Adana. Among them was my brother's son Krikor, the only one of that family left alive.

Turkish officials informed me that a girl from Kaisariya (now Kayseri) was staying at the home of the top government official mufti (judge) of the area. I immediately arranged to have her brought out and asked the kahana to counsel her. The girl was fifteen, and the mufti was planning to wed her later to his son who still was not mature. After three days, she, too, tried to escape, even though the kahana was taking excellent care of her in working to reconvert her. We suggested to gendarme Hovhannes of Zeitun that he marry her. This he did. She was with him when he later was transferred to Adana.

Toward the end of 1919, with conditions again getting dangerous, I sent Beatrice to Adana to be with her aunt Rahel. As the new year approached, I joined them. While I was there, Bishop Moushegh's younger brother, Vramshapouh Seropian, was making bombs in his house.

One of the bombs exploded accidentally; Vramshapouh and others were killed. The French military court found Bishop Moushegh guilty as an accomplice and sentenced him to death. Fortunately, he was able to escape to Smyrna.

—Vanished Hopes—

The thought that horror had ended for us was short-lived. The Kemalist movement, which began in the spring of 1919, saw to that. Again, massacres became the order of the day.

The rumors and indications were that the French had no intention of staying in Cilicia. Instead, they ultimately evacuated and turned the territory over to the Kemalists. There appeared to be a decision that Allied ends would best be met by permitting Kemal to build a strong new Turkey. And we had been looking forward to having in Cilicia an independent Armenian nation assured and backed by the Allied governments!

With an army available to him, and without interference from the French and other powers, Kemal thus was free to resume the Turkish slaughter of Armenians. This was motivated in part by his fear that our striving for independence posed a threat to him. Soon his fanatical guerrillas began terrorizing our communities. Though our soldiers put up brave resistance, the odds were overwhelmingly against them. Armenians again were dying by the thousands.

Who could describe the depth of our sorrow and disappointment? Were we forever to be the victims of Turkish hatred and butchery? We would survive as a people, yes.

We had survived before. But it was so difficult to bear this shattered dream, this dark chapter following so soon after the tragedy that had destroyed so much of our population.

For a time, the new massacres ceased. I returned to Osmaniye to see what the situation was there. What a shock I received! The Armenian marketplace and many homes had been burned, our house included. Those residents who remained alive were in a state of hopelessness. There appeared to be nothing I could do to help, so I went back to Adana.

In a short time, the Kemalists resumed the battles. Our badly outnumbered troops fought fiercely against them, but had little chance of stopping the onslaught. The catholicos went to Paris to seek help from the French, but returned empty-handed. Sis fell on June 7, 1920. Hajin, giving up fifteen thousand souls, suffered the same fate on October 15.

Beatrice and I had rented a room with her aunt in the parish of Tepe Bagh. Our situation was uncertain. We lived from day to day, unable to be definite about anything and wondering what the future held for us. Three happy things, however, did occur during this distressing period.

One afternoon I happened to meet gendarme Hovhannes of Zeitun in the marketplace. He insisted that I come to his house. I was delighted with what I found there. The girl from Kaisariya whom he had married after we liberated her from the home of a top Turkish official had just had a baby boy. She kissed my hand, expressing complete contentment and thanks for what we did to free her despite her resistance at the time. It was wonderful to see her so happy.

Then, some days later, my inseparable friend from

those anxious escapes during deportation, Ohan Karoghlanian, located me. He had a friend with him, Setrak Shamlian. They had come from Deortyol. How pleased I was to know Ohan was alive and to see him again. In recalling the experiences we had gone through together, we were all the more saddened that there appeared to be no way of halting the continued shedding of Armenian blood by the newly emboldened Turks.

The third event occurred on November 24, 1920. A daughter was born to us in our rented room in Tepe Bagh. We named her Armenouhi (Anna) and had her baptized at Saint Asdvadzadzin (Holy Mother of God) Church. Her godfather was Gaspar Arakelian, Rahel and Arakel's son, the boy I had enlisted to deliver meals at the German military hospital in Aleppo.

With a new baby to care for and with no relief from uncertainty in sight as the months went by, Beatrice and I faced a major decision. Two of her brothers, Nazareth and Joseph, had been in the United States for some time. After a long search through American missionaries, they had learned where we were living. And they were urging us to come to America. They even had gone so far as to send us official admission papers and money for passage.

It would be difficult to describe how emotionally torn I was in weighing and balancing what we should do. Armenians in Cilicia were in desperate need of help. From the time my mother had spoken to me as she lay near death, I had been devoted to helping our people whenever I could find a way of doing so. The reality was that under present conditions I could do pitifully little. Yet, was it right to leave them behind and pursue a new life in another land? Beatrice shared my emotions as I wrestled in my mind with that question.

Developments soon led me to a decision. There were rumors that secret talks were being held with the French to give Cilicia to the Turks. At the same time, the Turks began to bombard Adana with large cannon. It was clear that ongoing dangers confronted Armenian survivors of the four years of torture and suffering. At least in America my family would be safe. We would go there.

−A Long Journey−

We immediately began preparing to go to the Mersin seaport as the first destination in what was to be a lengthy trip. Beatrice's second cousin Jemelia had just married Abraham Der Stepanian, who had lived nine years in the United States. She pleaded with us not to go. "You are a teacher," she said to me. "You will never endure the life of a laborer in America. And that's what you will have to be."

Her words didn't deter me. "I shall break this staff of mine and leave it here," I answered. "In America, I shall be ready and pleased to do the most menial tasks to provide for my wife and child."

It was essential that we get to Mersin by railway before the routes closed. Thus we hurried our departure. We were joined by Nshan Der Bedrosian of Kharput who was to take three grown girls from the Benevolent Union orphanage with him to America. He would marry them to relatives there. For greater security, the orphanage had been transferred from Adana to Mersin.

Among the few things we had with us was a letter from Armenian leader Mihran Damadian, who had been imprisoned. The letter was to Boghos Nubar in Paris and concerned the frightful conditions of Armenians in Cilicia.

My eyes filled with tears as the train pulled away from Adana. I had hoped to place flowers on the graves of my parents and relatives for the last time. But this had not been possible. Leaving my birthplace where I had spent my childhood in the revered highlands filled me with deep emotion.

As the train gained speed, there began parading before my eyes the terrible events of the past few years, the unbelievable crimes that had obliterated so many innocent Armenians, the world's first Christian people: the four years of continuous deportation; the horrible massacres; the tens of thousands left to die at the sides of roads or thrown into the rushing waters of the rivers; the countless numbers cast away on mountain slopes or in deep ravines; the hundreds of thousands abandoned on endless parched desert sands; the young women and girls who threw themselves into the Euphrates and Tigris Rivers rather than yield to the Turks.

After we reached Mersin, I went to visit my godfather, Krikor Koudoulian, and bid him a last sad good-bye. I then went to the Benevolent Union orphanage to say my last farewells to the orphans I had placed there after rescuing them from Turkish homes.

On June 10, 1921, we took a ship from Mersin to Beirut. From there, we would go to America by way of France.

When we arrived in Beirut we went to the American consulate to have our passports certified. Then we returned to the ship, hoping to get to France soon. But this turned out to be a voyage that would visit many ports. It took eleven days to reach Marseille.

Our arrival in Marseille on June 21 was the beginning of

what was to become a two-week stay. We took a room at a hotel. Nshan Der Bedrosian, who previously had been in France as well as in America, served as our guide in seeing many places in the city. I'll never forget one afternoon when he suggested to me, smiling, that he and I go out together for a walk. He led me to a particular street. Suddenly a half-naked girl snatched my cap and said, "Bon, bon, venez ici," while trying to drag me to a building opposite. I was barely able to get my cap back.

"Nshan, was this your reason for proposing a walk?" I asked. He laughed, saying there were many other experiences I would have in the new world we were entering. "I brought you here purposely to this street of prostitutes so that you will understand some things about life in France."

With much love-making going on in public gardens we visited, it was obvious that permissiveness in sexual matters was part of France's renowned "Liberty, Equality, and Fraternity."

While we were in Marseille, we happened to meet the well-known patriot for the Armenian cause, Minas Cheraz, in a restaurant one day. He was not in good health. I told him of the bitter disappointment of our people in being abandoned by the French and again being made victims of the Turks. After listening for a while, he said with deep emotion: "From now on, the only hope of the Armenians is the Soviet Union, no matter what system of government they have. The physical survival of Armenians depends on the Soviets. The Armenians by now should have learned their lesson from the Western governments."

Was the Soviet Union to be the one hope for the Armenian people? There was much to think about in what he said.

We left for Paris about the beginning of July. Soon after

arriving, we delivered Damadian's letter to Boghos Nubar Pasha, president of the Benevolent Union. Then one day he held a tea for us at his residence. Other Benevolent Union officials were there. The entire conversation centered around what had befallen our people in Cilicia. It was agreed that something had to be done to protect Armenians from the ravages of the Turks. But what? A clear, reassuring answer was elusive.

After remaining in Paris for ten days, we were transported to Cherbourg to await our turn to embark for the United States. It wasn't until August 14, 1921, that we finally reached Ellis Island and had our entry examination. Beatrice's brother Joseph met us. We went from New York to Boston and were welcomed at the house of her brother, Nazareth Panosian.

It had been a long journey. But at last we were in our new land.

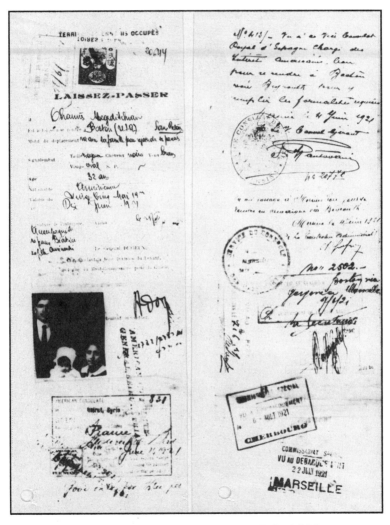

Our Passport Documentation, July 1921.

Beatrice, Anna, and I prior to sailing to America in 1921.

Beatrice's brother Joseph Panosian, circa 1921.

Beatrice's brother Nazareth Panosian, circa 1921.

Beatrice, Anna, and I in Boston in 1922.

–VIII–

Starting Over in America

Joseph didn't hold back in telling us how much money he and Nazareth had spent getting us to the United States. I assured both of them that I would work at any job I could get, no matter how menial it might be, to support my family and to repay the debt to them.

Within a week, Beatrice, our baby, and I had moved to an empty apartment belonging to Joseph. It was in Somerville, a short distance from Boston. The furnishings were sparse, but served our needs.

For four dollars a week, I went to work in a restaurant owned by an acquaintance of Joseph. My job was peeling potatoes and washing dishes. In those circumstances, I regretted having come to America. But my only choice was to adjust, continue on, and work hard to provide for my family.

It was plain that there was no way to support my family and repay Beatrice's brothers on four dollars a week. I heard that I might find better work in Watertown, where, I was told, some eight thousand Armenians were employed. Although Watertown was farther away—and it would be quite a distance to travel to and from there—I decided to look into it. So I went to talk with some Armenian barbers who had a shop in that locality.

One of the barbers, who was from Kharput, took me to a line of men applying for work at the Hood Rubber Company in Watertown. Because I did not know English, I would have to ask for a job by making signs with my hands.

My turn in the line was not reached that day, but I returned the following morning. When my turn did come, I began making gestures I thought would convey to the man doing the hiring that I wanted a job. He watched me for a minute or so, then made gestures with his own hands and said, "Go to hell."

My interpretation was that this meant I was to be hired. I went back to the Armenian barbers and told them I would be given a job the next day. They asked me how I knew I would have the job. "Because he said, 'Go to hell,' and I understood that to mean go away today and come back tomorrow to start your job," I explained. The barbers broke out into uncontrolled laughter. I asked them what I had said that was so funny. "He told you to get lost, that they had no work for you," they answered, still laughing. To that, I said, "So, if that's the way it is, I'll go again tomorrow and get a job."

The next day I again stood in line. After a while, I saw that the hiring man was looking at me and smiling. When my turn came, I said, "Armenian, Armenian," and made gestures meaning for him to hire me. He took my hand and led me inside. I was put into a cubicle, and with hand gestures, told to wait.

The wait was for a physical examination. Another Armenian applying for a job served as interpreter for the doctor who gave me a good bill of health. I then was taken to an Armenian from Constantinople with whom I would be working. It was heavy work. Twelve pairs of rubber shoes were lined on steel carriers. My job was to lift each set of twelve at one time and place the shoes on a conveyor. I started at twelve dollars a week, quite good compared with the restaurant's four dollars.

The next day I told my friends the barbers about my success. "That's amazing!" they said. "They tell you to go to hell and send you away, but you go back and get the job. Bravo! You are a man of will. You will succeed. Since you don't know how to lose hope, you can do anything." I was glad to hear those words of encouragement.

In traveling to and from work, I had to take several street cars, elevated trains, and subway lines. One evening when I was returning home I forgot to make a transfer at the right station. Changing back and forth I became utterly confused and had to ask fellow passengers for help. They could see I was a stranger unfamiliar with the language and helped me. It was one o'clock in the morning when I finally reached home. There was Beatrice sitting next to Anna's cradle, crying bitterly, thinking I had been the victim of an accident.

The next day I bought two dictionaries at the Berberian Bookstore, one translating Armenian to English, the other English to Armenian. It was obvious that I must learn English, and it was only right that I should get to know the language of the country that had accepted us.

—Changes, then Progress—

My job at the Hood Rubber Company in Watertown lasted only four months. Because it was necessary to cut back on production, I was laid off along with many of the other workers.

Soon, however, I got a job as dishwasher and chef's helper at the Mamigonian brothers' restaurant in the Jamaica Plain section of Boston. To be close to my place of work, we moved from Somerville to Jamaica Plain.

The restaurant had an Italian chef who didn't want to share any of his knowledge about cooking. But, anxious to learn, I took every opportunity I could to observe secretly how he prepared things. This went on for fourteen months until he was replaced by a Portuguese chef who had greater experience.

Meanwhile, on March 1, 1923, we were delighted to have a son born to us, Boghos (Paul). One of Beatrice's relatives, Haroutiun Kaljian, had bought an apartment building in Jamaica Plain. With our little family having increased, we moved into it.

The new chef was more friendly and taught me many things I wanted to know. He also told me he was hoping to get a position at the Hotel Plaza and that if he succeeded, he would take me on as second cook. A little later he was hired by that hotel as chef of its restaurant. I went with him at a salary of twenty-two dollars a week. He relied on me for many aspects of the food preparation and we had a most harmonious working relationship.

After fifteen months, unfortunately, the restaurant was sold to a Greek. All of us employed there, eighteen in number, were let go on the excuse that extensive changes and renovations were going to be made. The word was given to us on New Year's Day, 1924!

Instead of joy and happiness on that first day of the new year, there was sadness in our family. Without warning, I suddenly was out of work. But there was something that did give us comfort. Beatrice and I both were attending night school to learn English. Our grades were all A's.

Unemployment reached a high level in America in 1924. I was willing to do any kind of work I could get, but it was difficult to find anything. Luck came my way, however.

There was a factory near us that manufactured musical instruments of different kinds. Its owner was a Jewish immigrant from Germany, Mr. Bettoney. I decided to apply there.

The manager of the factory wanted to know what kind of work I could do. "I am not experienced in your work," I said, "but I am an Armenian. Show me any task, and if I can't carry it out, reject me." He asked me other questions, then said, "You appear to be a very unusual man. I'll try you out." He took me to the department of polishing, buffing, and plating, telling the supervisor to put me at a particular task. The foreman assigned me to polishing and trimming the keys that go on musical instruments. I passed the test and was hired.

Several months went by, but they would not let me move to any other kind of work. So I kept on with my assignment, making sure it was done quietly and effectively. There were eight workers in that particular department. The foreman, observing my work from a distance, noted how careful I was with it. He took an interest in me and learned that I was attending night school. To help me along, he gave me the opportunity to work two evenings a week overtime. I was happy to get the extra pay, and spending the two evenings did not interfere with attending school.

Most of the workers on our floor smoked (I was an exception). The floor itself was altogether uncared for and always in an unkempt condition. One day our foreman, after lighting his cigarette, tossed the match aside. The room, full of powdery work waste, immediately caught fire. Smoke went through the entire factory. Workers rushed in from all the other areas, and it took great effort to bring the fire under control.

The plant manager learned the cause of the crisis. And the next day I received a memorandum from him stating that, beginning the following day, I would be foreman of our floor. After reading it, I stood there somewhat stunned. The other workers noticed this. The present foreman came over, took the memorandum from me, and read it aloud. He was being transferred to the machine shop. How surprised I was! This responsibility was being given to me before I had completed my first year of work there.

As foreman, my first objective was to bring the work area into better order to avoid future fires and other possible accidents. I thought that suction fans on the machines could draw work waste through ducts to the outside. The waste would then be deposited in large tanks half full of water, making the whole plant safer and more healthy for the workers.

I presented this idea to the master mechanic. He assured me he could carry out the plan if it had the plant manager's approval. I went at once to the plant manager and explained the idea to him. After thinking for a moment, he complimented me and gave the plan his approval. I was rewarded with a fifteen-cent-an-hour increase in my wages.

To add to our happiness that my work was going well, another daughter was born to us. The date was March 6, 1925. We gave her my mother's name, Mariam (Martha).

After some time, I was able to pay in full my debt to my brother-in-law.

—A Matter of Duty—

Preoccupied as we were with our own affairs in America, I, nonetheless, could not ignore an opportunity, indeed what I considered a duty, to aid our people abroad.

It is important to recall what that great patriot for the Armenian cause, Minas Cheraz, said to us in Marseille when Beatrice and I were there on our way to America: "From now on, the only hope of the Armenians is the Soviet Union, no matter what system of government they have. The physical survival of Armenians depends on the Soviets."

How true that turned out to be. Out of the devastation the Armenian people had suffered, the one hope of rising as a cohesive homeland nation lay in Soviet Armenia. But the task of achieving this goal was tremendous.

In 1921, under the presidency of Hovhannes Toumanian, the H.O.G. (Hayasdani Oknoutyan Gomidé-Committee to Aid Armenia) had been organized as a non-political entity. Its purpose was to help in that building task. Michael Babashanian, who assumed the directorship, had issued this appeal:

O, all Armenians, wherever you are in the world, you are being called on by the H.O.G. You are being called on by the Conference of Armenian Workers and Armenian writers of all persuasions convened in the capital of Armenia. Do you not hear their united plea at this momentous juncture? Take note. After centuries of struggle, and worldwide upheaval, a free and independent Armenia is rising out of widespread calamity and misfortune. Heed the call from Armenia and rush to help in every way, to the extent, that you can.

At the same time, the famous Armenian historian Leo wrote of the situation this way:

Yes, we must help Soviet Armenia, generously and extensively. We have lost everything. There is left only a small Armenia, which today is exerting a supreme effort to free itself of loss of life from hunger, nakedness, and epidemic of disease as a result of years of overwhelming suffering. The present government of Armenia is working tirelessly and ceaselessly to restore as soon as possible that small piece of land allotted to us to a condition enabling economic progress and growth.

The H.O.G. began a worldwide operation, organizing branches in cities throughout the Soviet Union and in a number of other countries that included America, France, Bulgaria, Greece, Iraq, Egypt, and Lebanon. The committee actually became an official body representing the Armenian Republic in Armenian communities wherever they were in the world.

In 1923, committees were formed in America to raise money to help the struggling nation with agricultural machinery, tools, and tractors. The patriotic Armenians of Fresno, California, led the way in the money-raising activity. General Antranig, speaking at a meeting on the need to help the fatherland, personally contributed five hundred dollars. This action by the patriotic general so moved those present that they followed his example.

In the growing atmosphere of patriotism, we formed an H.O.G. branch in the Roslindale section of Boston. John Hovsepian and Mardiros Javian were the leaders. I was elected executive secretary.

The arrival in America in 1925 of a H.O.G. delegation coincided with worldwide news of the devastation caused by the Leninakan earthquake in the small Armenian nation working so hard to rise. Armenians in America began raising money from all who could give. Thanksgiving Day was close. I made an appeal through the Laper (Armenian) newspaper, asking Armenians everywhere to save by eating chicken instead of turkey and to do everything else they could to contribute to the aid of those suffering from the Leninakan catastrophe. Our H.O.G. branch did its share, serving as an example to other branches, which continued to grow as a result of Armenians' patriotism and generosity.

—More Changes—

At the end of April 1931, Beatrice and I were graduated from the Theodore Roosevelt Night School of Boston with high honors. John L. Mayor, superintendent of the school, congratulated us. A photograph of us appeared in the Boston Globe and other newspapers, along with a story commending us. A clipping from the Boston Globe has remained with us as a proud possession.

At that time, the owner of the factory at which I worked—Cundy Bettoney—opened a plant in Czechoslovakia to make parts for the musical instru-

*My wife, Beatrice, and I, with our children Anna,
Martha, and Paul in 1927.*

HUSBAND, 42, AND WIFE, 33, EVENING SCHOOL GRADUATES

MR. AND MRS. HOVHANNES MUGRDITCHIAN GRADUATES OF THEODORE ROOSEVELT SCHOOL BRANCH OF COMINS EVENING SCHOOL, ROXBURY

Of the graduates of the Theodore Roosevelt School branch of the Comins Evening School, Roxbury Crossing, last night a husband and wife were among the most interesting.

Hovhannes Mugrditchian, 42, and Mrs. Beatrice Mugrditchian, 33, had entered the school only last Fall, nevertheless, their attendance was perfect, and they had received "A"grades all along.

Mr. Mugrditchian was born in Armenia. He is a well-educated man, having attended school there and also high school in Jerusalem, which is on a higher student basis than the term "high school"signifies here. He was graduated from that institution at the age of 20.

For the following six years he taught school in his native country. He fought in the World War, and at its conclusion resumed his teaching. In 1921 he came to this country. He is employed as a foreman by a musical instrument concern in Boston.

He speaks Armenian, Arabic, Turkish and French fluently and is conversant with three other languages, he says.

He experienced little difficulty, because of his previous education and study of mathematics, the classics, Latin and Greek and the literature of the United States. In his current evening school work.

Both intend to go to high school, Mr. Mugrditchian, primarily to master the English language. After completing the high school course he hopes to study for either medicine or dentistry.

The Mugrditchians, who live at 384 Amory St., Jamaica Plain, have three children going to day school. They are Anna, 10, who is in the fifth grade at the Bowditch School; Paul, 8, who is in the third grade at the Hillside School, and Martha, 6, who is in the first grade at the Hillside School, in Jamaica Plain.

117

ments. Lower wages in that country would make his operations more profitable. Because they were incomplete items, the parts could be imported without duty and assembled in Boston into complete instruments. For the assembling, he kept only twelve workers in our factory, letting more than two hundred go. Our work area was closed entirely. I was without a job after having been there for eight years.

In remaining unemployed for a few months, I decided to learn a different skill so that I would have my own business. And, as I had said before we came to America, I wasn't particular about what kind of work it would be.

At the suggestion of friends, I went to a cobbler acquaintance, Paul Topjian, and offered to pay him something as well as work without income for a time if he would teach me shoe repairing. He agreed. After a period of learning other aspects, I asked him to let me work on the sewing machine. He refused, saying I would spoil the shoes. This annoyed me greatly, so much so that I left.

Another shoe repair shop in Roslindale was for sale. I scraped up enough money to buy it. The shop was equipped with new machines, and I started working resolutely to make the enterprise the success I was confident it could be. In the beginning, I would give those repair jobs that required sewing to a nearby friend, Garabed Konsolian, who was an expert at it. We split the profit. This went on for a while. In the meantime, I gained experience by taking my own old shoes apart and sewing them on the machine. Soon I was able to do all the work in the shop.

An Italian cobbler from not far away came in one day to discourage me. "I learned shoe repair when I was still in my mother's womb," he said. "You are just learning.

You will never be able to make a living here." I told him I would let the future determine that.

In fact, Germans and Italians in the area began coming to the shop, and I was satisfying them all by delivering good work.

Another day I had a surprise! Edward Gaben, manager of the musical instrument factory, came into the shop. He said that the plant opened in Europe by the owner had not been successful. The factory in Boston was to be improved and former workers were being offered their old jobs. "I would like you as an experienced supervisor to come and work with me," he said, "and I'll give you a raise." My answer was clear. "If you can guarantee me at least five years of work, I'll come." He was sorry that he could not offer me such a guarantee. Without that assurance, I was not willing to give up my shop and go.

With my own business proving to be successful, my greatest concern became that of giving my children an Armenian education. I wanted to open an Armenian school in Roslindale, the Boston suburb to which we had moved.

To bring into being a school of this kind, I knew my first need was to prepare an overall plan. Accordingly, I began spending evenings working on details. When my plan was completed, I sent it to the Armenian Diocese in New York. At that time, the primate of the diocese in the United States was Archbishop Ghevont Tourian. He returned the proposal fully approved.

With the effective help of Beatrice and others, we organized a women's league for the new school. Armenian families in Roslindale worked in unity and harmony to make its opening a success.

Unfortunately, however, unity and harmony did not last

in the Armenian community. Disruption came from a tragic event on Christmas Eve, 1933. During the divine liturgy at Holy Cross Church in New York City, the celebrant, Archbishop Tourian, was assassinated because of his support for the government in Soviet Armenia. The Armenian Revolutionary Federation was recklessly zealous in its determination to win independence for an Armenia entirely separated from the Soviet Union or any other nation. Armenians were dishonored by this tragedy.

Our school was affected because members of the Armenian Revolutionary Federation withdrew their children from it. But we did operate successfully for another five years. Among its graduates were our daughters, Anna and Martha.

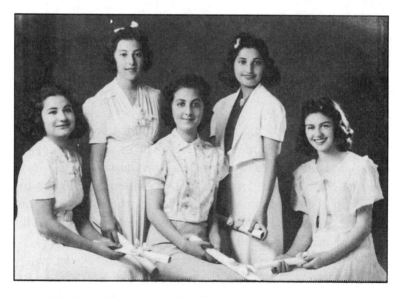

The first Armenian school graduating class (1935), Roslindale, Massachusetts. Our daughters Martha (first on left) and Anna (fourth from left) were among the graduates.

–IX–

Fulfilling a Vow

In 1935, great excitement prevailed as preparations were made to celebrate the fifteenth anniversary of the new Armenia. Delegations were being organized in America and other countries to go there for the celebration.

The H.O.G. selected me as one of the delegates from the Boston area. I could not decline the appointment even though I had a busy shop and responsibility for the livelihood of my family. The H.O.G. offered to cover my travel expenses, but I accepted only on the condition that I would assume these myself. I was remembering a vow I made before Der Bedros Vartabed Sarajian, superintendent of the seminary in Jerusalem (later bishop, and catholicos of Cilicia), when I was a student there: "I shall serve the Armenian people throughout my whole life, without asking anything in return."

Beatrice knew how strongly I felt about this and how anxious I was to go. She willingly volunteered to go to work to provide for the three children because it would be necessary for me to close the shop temporarily. I was most grateful for her understanding and help.

A delegation of thirty-two persons representing patriotic Armenian organizations in America left New York by ship on October 17, 1935. Accounts of the trip as it proceeded, written by Antranig Antreassian and me, appeared in the Lraper and the Baikar (Armenian) newspapers.

Arriving in London, we stayed there for a few days to visit interesting sites and museums. Then by ship for six days through the Baltic Sea we went to Leningrad. We were greeted there by a young man named Kevork Havhannesian who had been sent from Armenia. He was to accompany us to Yerevan.

We remained in Leningrad for nine days. Among many other sites, we visited the winter and summer palaces of the czars, now museums. A highlight was meeting the famous Armenian actor Vahan Papazian. We attended his performance of a Shakespearean play, and our delegation honored him with a bouquet of flowers.

From Leningrad we went by train to Moscow. We were received well there, saw beautiful dramas performed in the old Lazarian Academy, and visited important sites, including Lenin's Tomb.

From Moscow then, we traveled by train to Yerevan, the vibrant city in the new Armenia. There we were met by representatives of the H.O.G. and of the government. We were placed in the only hotel at that time, the Intourist, the manager of which was the poet-writer Soghomon Daronatsi.

Bishop Shahe Kasparian, a native of Aintab, had arrived earlier, and we unexpectedly ran into him at a restaurant. He and I had known each other in the Cilician catholicate of Sis when I was the teacher-superintendent of the seminary there from 1910 to 1912. After being in America for a period of time, he had just spent three years as superintendent of the Cilician catholicate in Antelias.

He had decided to return to America, but first wanted to visit the new Armenia. He was highly impressed with the efforts being made by the government to build a nation, however small, that would be a true homeland for Armenian people.

On the evening of November 23, he and others of us had dinner together at the Intourist Hotel restaurant. We talked late into the night. As we headed for our rooms, the bishop said to me, "Hovhannes, when we get back to America, I am going to shout from one end of the country to the other about the tremendous progress our people have made."

Sadly, he was not to fulfill that intention. Early the next morning, as he was going to the washroom, he had a heart attack and died. All of us were in deep grief. He was buried November 27 on the grounds of the Church of St. Gayane, next to Etchmiadzin.

We remained in Yerevan for twenty-eight days, visiting all the historical and important places. Everywhere we went we became fully cognizant of Armenia's exciting progress. The bishop would have been well justified in shouting about it from one end of the United States to the other.

On our return trip we visited a number of cities in the Ukraine—Khakov, Kiev, and others. We also went to Warsaw, Poland, where I was interested in learning about the Armenian community that once had been there. To my astonishment, I found that only seven families remained of an earlier Armenian population of one hundred thousand. And they were recent newcomers from Van. The old community had been drawn into the Roman Catholic Church and totally assimilated into the native population.

We reached Paris by way of Berlin on the last day of 1935. There we had meetings with the Central Committee of the H.O.G. By chance, I met a number of compatriots who suggested that we spend New Year's Eve together. I gladly agreed, and we had a most enjoyable time. After midnight I wanted to visit the Hotel New York where Beatrice and I had stayed when we were in Paris on our way to America. I was led to the hotel by the others. When we were in sight of it, they suddenly disappeared. Just in front of the subway entrance, two French women came up to me, tugged at my sleeve, and tried to get me to go with them. I got away from them and quickly was led into the hotel by the doorman. I became aware for the second time of the sexual leniency in France.

We arrived back in New York on January 10, 1936. The Central Committee of the American division of the H.O.G. asked me to spend at least two months as a field representative, visiting different states for the purpose of reestablishing H.O.G. branches that had disbanded and also organizing new branches.

Again, remembering my vow, I could not decline even though it meant keeping my shoe repair shop closed for an additional period of time.

—The Continuing Crusade—

My mission for the H.O.G. was not an easy one, but I pursued it earnestly. Although I was able to establish eight new branches in Chicago and surrounding areas, there was opposition from the working class of eastern Armenians.

The fact was that there were those Armenians who had

124

been misled, principally by the Armenian Revolutionary Federation, about the H.O.G. I had many arguments in trying to get them to understand the reality and truth. Often, but not always, I succeeded.

The underlying issue was politics. With the new Armenia being part of the Soviet Union, some insisted that those of us aiding the homeland were Communists perpetuating Communism. H.O.G. had nothing to do with politics. It was purely and simply an organization patriotically helping Armenians to establish their new homeland, the location of which was set by events for which world powers, not Armenians, were responsible.

In 1922 alone, H.O.G.'s early efforts had resulted in the following quantities of essentials being distributed in the new land:

• 1,160,000 pounds of flour
• 1,200,000 pounds of seeds
• 260,000 rubles worth of clothing
• more than 150 typewriters
• substantial sums of money for tractors and for reconstruction of earthquake-ravaged Leninakan

At the same time, repatriation of large numbers of Armenians was organized by H.O.G. branches. Patriotic unions, with the cooperation of the Armenian government, worked to build villages in the surroundings of the new capital, Yerevan. These were populated by thousands of refugees brought from Arapkir, Malatya, Marash, Zeitun, and other places in eastern Turkey.

By no means were these abundant contributions motivated by politics. On the contrary, it was entirely for humanitarian reasons that H.O.G. did so much to help the Armenian people at a time when help was so sorely needed. And I was pleased to have the opportunity of playing an active role in the efforts. But doing so proved dangerous for me.

After serving for a period as field representative for H.O.G., I reopened my shoe repair shop. In 1938, I had a chance to sell it and buy a grocery store. The idea of selling groceries appealed to me, and I made the necessary transactions to change my occupation accordingly.

Meanwhile, because of my work with the H.O.G., I had become an enemy of the Armenian Revolutionary Federation. On July 1, 1939, thieves broke into my store and ransacked it. Then, on January 13, 1941, two men entered the store and held me up, taking money from the cash register. As they left, one shot me with a revolver. Fortunately, a knife I carried in my shirt pocket deflected the bullet, but it penetrated my right side about an inch. I fell to the floor, but managed to get up and make my way to the telephone. I was taken to the hospital and had surgery that night.

My stay in the hospital lasted a month. While I was there, the police showed me photographs of many criminals. I recognized the man who had shot me, and a search was conducted for him.

Immediately after arriving home, I applied to the police for permission to purchase a gun for protection. Upon the recommendation of a detective working on the case, Mr. Hayim, I was granted this permission. I quickly bought a revolver, and I was lucky that I had.

One night not long after I was back in the store, I noticed three men standing out in front sizing things up. They obviously were making sure I was the only one inside. I soon recognized one of them as the robber who had shot me. I reached for my gun, pointed it in their direction, and called out, "Come on in. This time it's my turn."

The three men, seeing I was well prepared and armed, ran off to their car and drove down a one-way street. They abandoned the car and took off on foot. Based on further identification I was able to make of the one who had shot me, the police were sure that my assailant was a young man by the name of John McCarthy.

—More Moves—

In June 1941, our daughter Anna married Vagharsh Bedoian, who had just graduated from college. They moved to New Britain, Connecticut. At the same time, our son Paul was studying at an aviation technical school in Pennsylvania to become an aircraft and engine mechanic.

Not only friends, but the police warned me that I was in continuing danger of being killed by gunmen. We reached a decision that it was prudent to sell the store, though at a loss, and leave Boston. So that same year, 1941, we moved to New Britain, Connecticut. I obtained work at a submarine parts plant in nearby Plainville. World War II had begun in Europe.

My attacker, John McCarthy, was arrested in Boston, and I was called there for his trial, which began on March 18, 1942. My detective friend, Mr. Hayim, advised me not to be fooled by John McCarthy's appearance when I would be called on to identify him; he had grown a beard in the apparent hope I would not recognize him. The detective was German-born, and we respected each other. Sometimes we would converse briefly in German.

Before the trial actually got under way, several prisoners were brought into the courtroom. The judge asked me which one had shot me in the holdup at my store. I quickly pointed to the bearded John McCarthy. At the end of the trial, he sentenced the criminal to only five to seven years imprisonment. On hearing this unbelievably lenient sentence, I became extremely angry, and my teeth began to chatter. An Armenian friend wanted to know what was the matter with me. "Do you think this is just punishment?" I asked. "I was expecting at least ten to fifteen years would be given to the criminal."

We later learned that John McCarthy went blind. Although that is not a condition to wish on anyone, it seemed that retribution had made certain he would not attack others in the future.

Back at the plant in Plainville, eight persons were working in my group. One was an Italian under my supervision. His name was Hayastan. One day during lunch break I asked him how he got that name. He told me his family had decided that some member always must be named Hayastan (Armenia) so that Armenians and Armenia would not be forgotten. I recalled that after Cilicia had fallen, seventy thousand Armenian families had gone to live in Italy. This man named Hayastan belonged to one of those families. What a coincidence it was that we should be working together in faraway Plainville!

In 1943, our son Paul, who now was in the Army Air Force, was assigned to training close to New Orleans. It was at this time that Beatrice became ill. Doctors recommended that for her health we should move to a mild climate in California. We made a decision to do so, and went to Los Angeles by way of New Orleans to spend a few days visiting our son.

Beatrice's cousin, Jack Panosian, and his family lived in Los Angeles. We stayed with them for two weeks while we looked for a house. We found one, which we rented and moved into immediately. I applied for work at North American Aviation. With excellent references from the plant in Plainville, I was accepted at once. I applied myself heart and soul to the work. And how proud I was to be honored with a card bearing President Roosevelt's signature attesting to my being the factory's best worker in class two, heavy work. A welcomed increase in pay came with it.

Our family was an active part of the war effort throughout World War II. Paul was transferred to Florida where he was assigned duties performing heavy aircraft maintenance. Our older daughter Anna was a senior secretary for the navy. Martha, our younger daughter, was working as a navy inspector. And I was at North American in Los Angeles. My work there ended with the close of the war in August 1945. I was among some twenty-three thousand workers who were released. It was time for me to retire.

All of us were pleased to have been able to do our share to help achieve victory for America and her allies. What was accomplished on the home front in this great nation rightfully was called a miracle of production.

We were able to buy a duplex house on Seventh Avenue. Once moved in, I set about pursuing a number of my hobbies.

—Armenia Beckons—

The Armenian National Council planned and organized an International Armenian congress, which convened in

New York in April 1947. I was one of the delegates selected by the California National Council to attend this important affair.

There were 707 delegates from America. They came from seventy-six cities in sixteen states. Sixty-two representatives from twenty-two foreign countries also were present, as were representatives of leading Armenian churches and other organizations.

The congress opened on April 30 with an impressive banquet at the Waldorf-Astoria Hotel in New York. Speakers included Nshan Shahinian, chairman of the National Council; Professor H.M. Dadourian, who served as master of ceremonies; primate of the American diocese Archbishop Tiran Nersoyan; U.S. Senator Charles U. Tobin; Gen. Haig Shekerjian, the only Armenian general in the U.S. Army; Dr. Raymond Walsh, a well-known radio analyst; and Edwin Smith, chairman of the American Committee for the Defense of Armenian Rights.

The sessions also took place at the Waldorf-Astoria. They, too, featured many Armenian notables from various parts of the world.

The highlight of the congress was the reading of the historic Gontag (Encyclical) that had been written on April 20, 1947 and signed by the Catholicos of All Armenians, Gevorg VI. In clear language, this hallowed patriarchal message set forth the just rights of the Armenian people. It called on Armenians to work for repatriation to their homeland, and for efforts to regain expropriated native lands.

The influence this document had on the congress was reflected in the decisions reached by the delegates. One was to further repatriation in every way possible, with craft guilds to be formed by repatriates for the specific purpose of building the economic strength of the homeland. Another was to undertake fund-raising to provide additional aid.

The congress closed on Sunday, May 4, with a tremendous meeting in Carnegie Hall. Among those present was the daughter of the late President Woodrow Wilson. She spoke in most moving terms of her father's fervent desire that there be justice for the Armenian people with respect to their homeland. She earned the applause and esteem of the entire audience of some three thousand people.

Two days later, on May 6, I was one of a 110-person delegation to visit President Franklin Roosevelt's grave in Hyde Park, New York. A beautiful floral wreath was placed on the grave while Der Garabed Kahana of Tadem recited appropriate prayers. Then we visited the former residence of the Roosevelts, as well as the library, which had become an American pilgrimage site.

The congress had been an historic event in the experience of the Armenian people. It was the first time such a large and widely representative gathering had taken place in Armenia's behalf. I returned to Los Angeles deeply impressed by the meeting itself and by the Gontag of His Holiness, Catholicos Gevorg VI. I thought of selling our house, forming a craft guild, and repatriating to Armenia. It would be an opportunity to do more towards fulfilling my mother's request and my own vow to devote myself to helping our people.

There, with my own hands, I could build a home, hoping that in time our children would join us and work there alongside us. I was thinking that if Armenians from all over would go to Armenia and use their abilities, skills, and experiences, our fatherland would progress and prosper like America.

– X –

Facing New Realities

Shortly after the congress ended, the first group of repatriates was being organized in America. They would leave for Armenia later in 1947. A second group would depart in 1948.

Beatrice was fully aware of my feeling about going to the homeland, and she wanted me to be satisfied. At the time, she was a forelady in the sewing department of a leather goods factory. She was an expert at it. Women working under her supervision made a variety of men's and women's leather items—wallets, handbags, key holders, and the like. The logical thing for us was to form a guild of leather workers. By doing so, we could be part of the second group of repatriates in 1948.

Through an article in the Lraper newspaper, I issued a call for men and women to join us in creating a leather-working guild. A minimum of four to five members was needed. After some time, Haig Stamboulian and his family of New York and Mrs. Vartouhi Magarian of Los Angeles responded. We had our required number.

It was essential that one be competent in the use of all kinds of machines and tools used in the craft. To accomplish this, I went to the owner of the factory where Beatrice worked and offered to serve entirely without pay if he would allow me to work with the equipment.

He, a Jewish immigrant from Germany, was a fine man. He agreed to the proposition, and I began to work freely in the factory. The owner had such a favorable feeling toward us that he gave Beatrice a key to the factory so we could work there after hours. In a few months, I managed to become quite proficient in the use of the machines and tools.

Beatrice and I, Los Angeles, 1948.

Our home on Seventh Avenue, Los Angeles, 1948.

When this point was reached, I put our two-family house on Seventh Avenue up for sale. In a newspaper ad I stated that I wanted to sell to an Armenian, at a minimum price, so an Armenian would benefit. Japanese and Chinese persons offered to pay $22,000, but I declined those offers and sold the house to G. Terzian for $14,500.

After the sale was made, Beatrice went to New York to make necessary purchases of household items we would need in Armenia. I had to remain behind to complete final details of the real estate transaction.

It was a coincidence that while all this was going on the owner of the factory where we had been working decided to sell his machinery and tools. He wanted to go into a different business. I took advantage of the opportunity to buy the various pieces, including leather-cutting dies, and had them shipped to New York. I then went east myself, hoping we could go with the second group of repatriates to Armenia.

After I arrived in New York, we finished buying furniture and other household goods that we would need. We did this through an acquaintance, Albert Janjigian. We paid him five thousand dollars. The idea was to benefit an Armenian rather than a stranger by making the purchases through him. It was a reflection of the unbounded desire I had to help Armenians in every way possible.

Sad to say, we were deceived. When the shipment arrived in Yerevan, items were missing. Obviously Janjigian had not bought them at all. Others who purchased supplies through him had the same experience. Blinded by greed, so-called patriots like Janjigian revealed their true colors.

—A Long Wait—

The Soviet ship designated for us was scheduled first to transport repatriates from Egypt to Batumi (in Georgia on the Black Sea). Then it was supposed to come to America to take our group. But misfortune struck the vessel! It caught fire and burned at the seaport of Odessa as it was on the way from Batumi.

We thus had to wait for another ship. It, however, was delayed, then not sent at all. An announcement came that the repatriation would cease. By that time, our wait had extended to months. We sent a delegation to the Soviet Embassy to complain, pointing out that we had sold our homes and could not return to them.

Most of the people in our group had been living at a

hotel in New Jersey. We, however, were staying in a rented room in New York. While we waited, Beatrice busied herself developing the skill of sewing gloves. She became very adept at the technique.

After waiting a long time, we received word from the Soviet Embassy that if we insisted on repatriating, we would have to travel at our own expense to the seaport of Naples in Italy. A Russian ship would pick us up there and transport us to Batumi. From there it would be possible to travel by rail to Soviet Armenia.

Friends tried to persuade us not to repatriate at this time in view of all the problems we were having. They suggested we wait a few years and even said they would join us then if we did. We had sold our house; how could we change our minds now? We had made sacrifices to go. I was determined that we would get there. We would not retreat from our purpose.

Our group of repatriates had to hire the Gdynia Lines ship Sobieski in order to get to Naples. I paid eight hundred dollars for the two of us. About fifteen persons among our group withdrew from the repatriation. One was Karekin Antigian of Los Angeles who had joined our guild after its initial organization.

Finally, after going through a number of government inspections, we boarded the Sobieski on a misty Friday morning. It was January 21, 1949. There were 158 in our group of repatriates.

Our supplies were to remain in a warehouse for shipment to us by the repatriation committee in New York. The goods Beatrice and I had assembled included one Willys automobile, all the machinery and tools for the guild, and a large quantity of leather. For building our home in Yerevan I had procured eleven doors for a seven-room house, window frames and large crates of window glass, bathroom fixtures, a forty-gallon electrically heated tank for hot water, a washing machine, a stove, electrical appliances, and other items normally found in American houses. To ship all these materials, I had a number of large metal chests built at a cost of six hundred dollars.

As we settled into our cabin on the Sobieski, Reverend Aznakian, a highly respected New York clergyman, came to say good-bye. I had met him at the 1947 congress and had visited with him several times during our long wait for transportation across the Atlantic. He asked me to be sure, once we were in Armenia, to go to the Catholicos of All Armenians and discuss with him an important matter dear to the heart of this patriotic minister. It concerned celibacy.

He pointed out that the practice of celibacy had entered the Armenian church under pressure from outsiders. "If celibacy is removed," he said, "we unfortunate separated Protestants, together with all of our faithful, promise to return to the bosom of the Armenian church. And as religious workers in the fold, we will toil for the betterment of the Armenian church and the Armenian people."

We were to discover, however, that conditions prevailing within Armenia made it impossible to carry out his request.

After a comfortable voyage that lasted two weeks, we arrived in Naples and took rooms in a hotel. A week later, we boarded a Russian freighter that took us on a slow trip to Batumi. There we were met by a group of people sent by the Armenian government. They escorted us by rail to Yerevan. We arrived there on Beatrice's birthday, Friday, February 26, 1949.

—Life in Yerevan—

In Yerevan some of our group were settled in regular residential buildings. Others of us were placed in dormitory-like structures. These had no drinking water or toilets. We had to go quite a distance to get water and carry it back.

Beatrice and I became neighbors of several families who had come earlier from Egypt. Our supplies still were in New York waiting for a Russian ship to transport them to Batumi. Then they would come by rail to Yerevan. Meanwhile, the government gave each person 150 rubles for necessities.

It was a misfortune for all of us that the winter of 1949 was unusually severe. Snow and ice were everywhere, and it was bitter cold. The dormitory rooms assigned to Beatrice and me were in wretched condition, making matters worse. When it rained, the water leaked in all around and we had to take refuge in neighbors' rooms. The Tahmizian family from Egypt, staying next door to us, wanted to be of help until our things arrived. They gave us a bed and bedding to protect us from the cold.

Under these conditions, Beatrice became extremely disheartened and fell sick. Her blood pressure rose very high, and her heart began to weaken. I constantly was running to a nearby clinic to plead for help from the head nurse, Miss Nevart, to save my wife's life. She would run back to our billet and give Beatrice injections to strengthen her heart. This magnificent nurse was a repatriate from Greece. Her sister, Mrs. Azniv Ohanian, was the doctor's wife.

During this distressing time, Beatrice often would say to me, "Let me die, and be freed." And I would answer,

"I did not let you die in the Arabian deserts. Would I let you die here? No, I will not let you die. Don't lose hope. You will get well."

The miserable conditions persisted for quite a while. Finally, the weather changed. The warm sun melted away the snow and ice. How happy we were that Beatrice began to get well.

Another happy event occurred a little later. One day we went to visit our friend Haig Stamboulian. He was living on the second floor of a two-story building across from the bus station. There we met a man by the name of Karamanougian, of Aintab, who had come to see Haig. He asked Beatrice which family of Aintab she belonged to. When she told him she was from the Der Boghosian clan, a great smile crossed his face. "Your sister is here with her family, children, and grandchildren," he said.

We were taken by total surprise! "Which sister?" Beatrice asked excitedly. He said it was Srpouhi and that she was living near us in the third section. Beatrice was so anxious to see her that I said I would go at once with Karamanougian and get her. Srpouhi, as excited and anxious as Beatrice when we told her we had come to get her, came back immediately with us. We were deeply moved by the embrace of the two sisters. They had not seen each other since they were children. Their love for Armenia had brought them together.

We had met Srpouhi's husband, Stepan Frankian (formerly Demirjian), in Aleppo when both Beatrice and I had found refuge there many years before, but Srpouhi was not with him. Because he was a famous ironsmith, the Turks had kept him in Aleppo as an important craftsman for them. The entire family had repatriated to Armenia with the first caravan from Beirut in 1946, with children and grandchildren they numbered nearly eighty persons. This unexpected and joyous development meant a great deal to Beatrice and helped immeasurably to restore her health.

We had not anticipated that the people of Armenia would be living under such mean conditions as we experienced during that year, 1949.

Armenia had provided two hundred thousand young men to military service during World War II, and more than half had lost their lives. On the streets were mainly older persons and orphaned children. The repatriates were trying to ameliorate this sad situation in whatever ways they could. The painful truth was that the country had sacrificed a large part of its resources to help bring about victory in World War II.

Besides a severe shortage of housing, food was insufficient, thus it was rationed. For example, one day I had been standing in line for two hours to buy bread. When my turn came at the counter, I was informed by the clerk that it was all gone. The next morning I had to be in line before dawn so that I might buy our day's supply of bread. Often, not able to get real bread, I would have to settle for soukharin, a dry bread similar to toast. And one time we found it was moldy; we had to throw it away in a stream.

When riding on the train, we would see large white lice running around on the outer garments of the passengers, seemingly racing one another. I did not want to sit, and always rode standing. The shortage of soap was horrible. Beatrice and I were fortunate to an extent; we had brought a good supply of soap and some other necessities. The soap shortage continued for years until a soap factory finally opened in Yerevan.

With so many shortages, it was not surprising that there

was an active black market in Yerevan. It was called sev shouga. On Sundays, people would rush to a site where they were free to sell things at any price they wished or to buy things they needed if they had the money to pay exorbitant prices for them. American nylon stockings sold for 150 rubles, a phenomenal price. A man's outer shirt sold for 300 rubles. People came from Georgia and Azerbaijan to buy merchandise. Armenian items were in special demand.

I would go to the black market on Sundays to sell some of our clothes so that we might have a minimum daily sustenance.

—Living in Fear—

It was hardly a month after our arrival in Yerevan that rumors began to fly among the repatriates. And there was growing evidence that they were well founded.

Stalin had promulgated a new constitution for the Soviet republics. This prescribed that no Soviet nation or region had a right to declare itself a government if it had a population of less than one million. Instead, it must become part of an adjacent republic. Just as he had done with the lands of the Osseti and Abkhazi peoples, his plan was to annex Armenia to his own fatherland, Georgia. To keep our population at a level that would permit him to carry out his plan he exiled repatriates to Siberia for the flimsiest of reasons.

As a result, Stalin's secret agents lurked everywhere. They had been instructed that repatriates suspected of disloyalty to Moscow were to be arrested during the night, thrust into the "black auto," and taken to the railway station. There they would be crowded into freight cars and exiled to Siberia.

A manhunt, full of terror, had begun. It was carried out in the middle of the night so that neighbors would not see it. People would get up in the morning and find that neighbors had disappeared.

A repatriate who had come from America in 1936 and was teaching English at the Foreign Language Institute advised that if anyone were to come to see us and try to obtain information, we should remain silent. "Just listen," he said. "Express yourselves with hand motions only. Keep your eyes open and your mouths closed. Stalin's agents lurk everywhere, all about you. If they hear any little complaint or dissatisfaction issuing from your lips, they will arrest you and send you to Siberia. For your safety's sake, do what I say."

That warning so sincerely and earnestly given to us proved to be our salvation during the Stalin regime.

Terrible apprehension and fright arose among the repatriates. They began to isolate themselves, not mixing with one another, not talking, not being seen with relatives and friends. In fact, members within families even began to fear and suspect one another.

One example illustrates the terrible situation that prevailed. It happened to the expatriate father of the teacher who had given us such good advice about being cautious and silent.

The father had been exiled to Siberia. His two youthful sons did now know why. Both sons were conscripted into the army in 1941. One died a hero's death on the battlefield. The other, our friend, had saved the life of a Russian general in battle. After the war, the general asked him what he could do to repay him. The young man said he wanted nothing other than to know the crime for which his father had been exiled to Siberia. The general answered that it was a difficult request, but he would try to honor it.

After making an extensive investigation over a period of time, the general gave the young man the answer: "My son, your father's crime was to say, 'It will take one hundred years for this country to catch up with America.'"

That was the way life was for the people of Armenia during Stalin's days when more than sixty-five thousand innocent Armenian repatriates were crowded into freight cars and exiled to Siberia. Under such conditions, there was no way I could fulfill Reverend Aznakian's request in New York that I go to the Catholicos of All Armenians in Etchmiadzin and discuss with him the subject of celibacy.

—Our Goods Arrive—

When our things finally arrived from America, it took several days for them to be inspected before they were delivered to us.

When the inspection came to my books that had been shipped, the examiner put many of them aside, leaving only dictionaries. Included in those removed was the latest comprehensive work on the history of the church and theology by the famous patriarch of Constantinople, Archbishop Maghakia Ormanian, a work I had not yet read. As explanation for keeping the books, the examiner said, "Comrade Mugrditchian, you are just one person. We are going to place these books in the government library so that thousands will read them and benefit. You will excuse us." All I could say was, "Let it be as you wish."

It took another several days for large trucks to deliver to us the twenty-two crates of machines and tools for the guild, our household goods, the Willys automobile, and other large boxes. All were placed outdoors alongside our dormitory. There was no available building in which to put them. This remained the situation until we were able to build our own residence and move everything there.

Cars were very scarce in Yerevan in 1949. Although a number of repatriates had brought their cars, they had only limited use of them because of the difficult conditions that prevailed. I was no exception. And since there were opportunities to sell cars, particularly to government officials from Georgia and Azerbaijan, I decided to dispose of our Willys.

The overall inspector of automobiles was a high-ranking military man named Karamov, an Assyrian Armenian. Taking advantage of his position, he was buying cars for paltry sums and selling them clandestinely for prices five to six times higher. Fortunately, I had been told about this and knew I should not sell to him.

Government officials from Georgia and Azerbaijan offered a high price to me for the Willys, which was still in its crate. They also made a proposal to transfer us to Azerbaijan to start up our leather shop there, promising free residence, all kinds of conveniences, and other benefits. I thanked them for their generous offer, but declined. After all, I had come to help Armenia and would be going back on my promise by going elsewhere.

An Armenian long established in Yerevan offered to buy the car for twenty thousand rubles. I agreed and naively mentioned it to a neighbor Armenian, a repatriate from New York. He went at once and informed Karamov.

Early the next morning, two policemen came and took the Willys to Karamov. When I went to him and asked that the car be returned to me, he said threateningly, "You are not allowed to sell an automobile without my knowledge." He asked me to return the next morning. When I did, he took me to a bank office. There he said he would pay me ten thousand rubles and the car would be transferred to him. He added that he knew I needed the money. I told him I would not sell to him at that price. But he refused to offer anything more. And he did not allow me to take the car home.

Every day I went to his office and tried to get the car. But he refused to release it to me. One day his driver said to me secretly, "Don't you know you're in danger of having some men come at night, put you in a black auto, and exile you to Siberia? Your only recourse is to agree with Karamov. I am telling you this for your own good. Take whatever he offers you for the car."

My answer was, "I have worked without pay for years to help the people of Armenia. Let them put the traitors in the black auto."

Among the people who had come to meet us in Batumi on our way to Yerevan were two men who had taken a special interest in me. They had told me that if at any time I had difficulty in Yerevan to let them know, that they would do whatever possible to help me. But I had lost their addresses. Oh, how I wished I could locate them!

What good fortune I had! One day as I was nearing Karamov's office trying to figure out how to free myself from the car headache, I happened to meet one of those two men. I was overjoyed to see him and shook his hand warmly. He wanted to know why I had been looking so dejected. "Comrade Haroutiunian," I said, "I have a great problem." And I explained the whole matter to him. His words comforted me. "Don't lose hope," he said. "Now that we have met again, I am going to help you."

Taking my arm, he led me to Karamov's office. The traitor from New York was there, seated next to Karamov. My friend, an official, began to speak, very firmly. He berated Karamov. "These people have worked hard and sacrificed freely for our fatherland," he said, "And you, a good-for-nothing, want to rob patriots like Comrade Mugrditchian."

Karamov's face flushed and he squirmed in his chair. The traitor, the neighbor who had told Karamov about the offer I had for the car, squirmed with him. I went home hoping that at long last I would get out from under this problem that had been plaguing me.

The patriotic official who had come to my rescue was born and reared in Russia. His parents had come from western Armenia. He later had moved to Armenia where he obtained a good position and learned Armenian. The day after our meeting, he informed the appropriate ministry of Karamov's secret deals and cheating of repatriated Armenians. He asked that there be a trial and punishment.

Early the next morning, Karamov sent his driver for me. When I arrived at his office, he locked the door, asked me to forgive him, and offered me eighteen thousand rubles for the car instead of ten thousand rubles. I agreed. He counted out the money and asked me to sign a receipt, which I did. His driver then took me home safely.

Karamov quickly was subjected to an investigation by the Ministry of Unlawful Activity. In a few weeks, I was called to court. When I arrived at the building to which I had been summoned, many others were there, standing at the front door and elsewhere outside. I asked a woman why we had been called.

"They want us to testify," she answered. "Karamov framed my husband and had him tried and sentenced to eight years of exile in Siberia. And he frightened many into giving up their cars cheaply so he could sell them underhandedly to others at high prices. We have been called to tell of these things."

As I stood beside a stairway at the entrance to the building, a black automobile drove up. Karamov, hatless, was removed from it. Seeing this miracle, I said to myself, "Ah, that man who might have had me placed in a black auto and exiled to Siberia has now himself sat in a black auto, and God is punishing him."

At the trial, all those who had problems with Karamov were called on, one after another. At the end, the judge gave his verdict: "Karamov is guilty of illegal activity. He will be stripped of all his military honors and his party membership. He will be imprisoned for five to seven years."

The verdict was greeted with a sigh of relief by those who had suffered from Karamov's greed and abuse of power.

–XI–

Getting Settled

The government assigned lands free to repatriates who wanted to build houses. Also, the banks advanced twenty-five thousand rubles for each structure. In addition to the property set aside for the building itself, adjacent land was designated for use as individual gardens for vegetables and fruit trees.

We could not stay indefinitely without necessary conveniences in our dormitory residence. We had shipped from America the needed equipment—doors, windows, plumbing, electrical, and other building supplies—for erecting a place of our own. Before setting up our craft guild, we had to have a suitable place to live.

With this objective, I began to search for a desirable plot of land. After much effort, I found a site on Baghramian Boulevard, an elevated plot quite suitable for building a four-apartment structure. A foundation already had been laid but had been abandoned.

The property belonged to a military officer who had been transferred to Moscow. His father, however, remained in Yerevan. The place was for sale, and the value of the foundation structure was nine thousand rubles. But the father wanted twenty thousand rubles. The site appealed to me very much. Its location on high ground offered a view of the whole city. The plains of Ararat all the way to Etchmiadzin, as well as Ararat itself, were in clear view.

Two persons, Vahan Magarian and Siragan Soukiasian, both repatriates from America, joined me to purchase the foundation. We paid the twenty thousand rubles, but were given a receipt for only nine thousand rubles to comply with regulations. Word leaked to the government that we actually had paid more. Before long, the military man's father and I were called into court on the grounds that a bribe had been paid to procure the land. When I showed my receipt for nine thousand rubles, however, the court let us go free.

—Construction Project—

I took the responsibility for securing the government loan and all other matters pertaining to the building of the structure we visualized. Once the preliminary details were resolved, I set out to find an expert in building houses. After considerable search, I found such a man, an Armenian from Bulgaria named Kevork. Only after examining other structures he had built and obtaining further information about him did I decide to go ahead with him. We agreed that for forty-nine thousand rubles he would build all the main walls and the roof of the four-apartment building, which also would have a cellar with a ceiling height of at least three meters. The interior details of the structure were to be left to each of us who had joined in the purchase.

The agreement was signed with the provision that the builder would proceed and, without interruption, complete the structure we had specified. In a few days, his crew was at work to construct the walls.

After six months of work, the builder presented me with a request for ten thousand additional rubles for building balconies not included in the initial plans. We agreed to pay that additional amount, bringing the total cost to fifty-nine thousand rubles.

As soon as the walls and roof of the building were completed, we started on our interior work. The first step was to provide water and electricity. The electrical work was done by two repatriate electricians from America, Antranig and Freddy Aslanian. We, of course, had shipped the electrical supplies and equipment from America. Next we set about building the partitions for our separate apartments and rooms.

Beatrice and I chose our apartment to be on the second floor, east side. Magarian selected the apartment below ours, Siragan Soukiasian the second floor, west side.

Our apartment had a large balcony on the east and a medium-sized balcony overlooking Baghramian Boulevard. I arranged to have a young artisan repatriate from France—his name was Arshag—work with me to complete the interior structural details. He was skilled in carpentry, masonry, and other needed crafts. The two of us worked hard to finish as soon as possible.

I noticed that nearly every day at lunch break, Arshag, even though he was earning very good wages, ate only onions, garlic, and dry bread. I asked him why. With deep emotion, he told me about his family problems.

Arshag had married a Russian woman who had a fifteen-year-old daughter from a previous marriage. All his earnings were going to the woman and her daughter. They, enjoying many luxuries, allowed him only onions, garlic, and dry bread. I was grieved on hearing his sad story and began to share my midday meal with him. Then one day when he arrived for our usual work, I could see that he was extremely dejected. He frankly related an episode of the evening before. He had complained to his wife about the way she was treating him. She immediately took up a large knife from a table and went after him with it. Barely able to escape, he had spent the night at a neighbor's house.

Arshag's plight greatly perturbed me. I saw to it that he would not again have to face that vicious woman. He would sleep nights in our building, since we already had water, plumbing, electricity, and other conveniences. We also helped him to get a divorce from her.

It took four months to finish the interior work of the building. At about that time we learned through acquaintances of a very fine woman whose husband had died during the war and who was living in the third section of Yerevan. She had her own small residence with a plot of land adjacent. One Sunday I went to visit her. She was from Iran, and I found her to be a splendid person. We arranged to have Arshag marry her.

Arshag by then had earned four thousand rubles for his work. So two rooms were added to her house, and since he was a skilled artisan, other facilities were improved. A year later, they were blessed with a baby boy. This newly formed and happy family invited me to their home many, many times to express their appreciation for my having freed Arshag from his miserable existence, enabling him to have a family.

Thanks to our incessant toil, we were able to complete

our apartment and move in on November 5, 1950.

The cellar of our building was divided into two large sections separated by a wall. The height of the ceiling was three and one-half meters. I was able to place many of the materials of our craft guild and some of the machinery into one of the sections. The other, on the north side, we converted in such a way that it could be rented out, since it had all the conveniences of separate entrance, water, windows, etc.

—New Hurdles—

Magarian and I had agreed earlier that I would have free use of the lower passageway from his part of the yard to mine because the entire northern wall of the building was constructed heavily and solidly. When I wanted to go out to my yard one day, I found he had built a wall to close off the passageway. The result was that I had to hire a master mason, Garabed Chakmakjian, to cut an opening in the outer wall so that we had a separate entrance/exit for our garden. I also had to add some steps. This added work cost another fifteen hundred rubles.

Moreover, without our permission, Magarian took the ten thousand rubles we received for selling the fourth apartment in our building to a teacher named Mekenian. He refused to pay Siragan Soukiasian and me our rightful shares, using such baseless reasoning as, "It is said that if you must know your friend, you must do business with him."

Because Magarian committed such ungrateful and underhanded acts, Soukiasian and I cut our social relationship with him. I had done all the work in buying the land, getting the government loan, supervising the construction of the building, and carrying out a variety of other responsibilities. All this extended over a period of months and I did it willingly without receiving a kopek from the others who would share the building.

My plot of land, a large field, was on the north side of the building. I started to clean it up and put it in order by removing rocks and having truckloads of topsoil brought in. Also, I built a wall surrounding the plot and had outdoor plumbing installed. Then I built a bench that would seat several persons. When I tired from working in the garden, I could rest there.

My first action in cultivating the land was to plant three kinds of mulberry trees; later I would graft on still other varieties. Next I planted two kinds of apricot, followed by plum, wild cherry, fig, and other fruit trees, as well as twelve varieties of grape. A separate area was set with strawberries, and the rest of the land was to be for vegetables.

One day Sarkis Kurkjian was helping me with work in the garden. A fine man, he was the husband of a niece of Beatrice's. Suddenly, as we were working, I felt a terribly intense pain in my right knee. Sarkis struggled hard and managed to get me up to our apartment. On the knee was a walnut-sized swelling. I couldn't even bend my leg. Doctors were called. They advised that I be taken to a hospital for surgery.

Fortunately, we learned of an elderly sunukji (old-fashioned, home-grown chiropractor) named Hasekian, a repatriate from Aleppo. He had worked in a local hospital for quite a while, but now was retired. We called on this experienced man to examine my knee. He studied the condition and said, "My son, this is a rich man's ailment.

Do not rub it. You must keep water from gathering on the knee. Give it exposure to the sun, or regular fifteen-minute exposure to an electric lamp. In time it will go away the same way it came."

His advice was followed to the letter. In a month and a half the swelling first shifted location, then disappeared. We gave thanks to this skilled repatriate whose advice saved me from further complications.

—The Craft Guild—

We had come to Yerevan to make leather items that would benefit life for the people of Armenia and would aid in development of the struggling nation's economy. We had been led to believe we would have full encouragement and cooperation. Otherwise we would not have set out to organize such a guild while we were still in America, nor would we have made a large investment in equipment and supplies to be shipped to Yerevan. Yet, our efforts to proceed met with nothing but disappointment and frustration.

Despite constant appeals to the Ministry of Industry, we could not obtain permission to establish our planned manufacturing operation. Furthermore, we were not allowed to sell our equipment and supplies to a local leather calendering factory eager to procure them in order to produce new and better leather goods.

Beatrice and I were more than willing to make samples of leather items; she was an expert in this art, and technicians in the calendering factory were anxious to learn from her. I too was ready to teach the technicians how to use our machinery and equipment. But government officials turned aside our offers, ignoring sacrifices we had made

Grapes from our backyard vineyard in Yerevan.

My relative Vartevar Mugrditchian with me in the garden.

for the benefit of our fatherland. The whole thing was a complete riddle to us, totally beyond understanding. Finally, however, it was brought to our attention that Stalin's men had their eyes on us. It was clear that we had better become silent and hope for better days later.

Meanwhile, I could not continue to be unemployed. We had been living on the proceeds of selling clothing and other materials we had brought over with us. But we were running out of them. I needed to get a paying job to provide for our livelihood. The director of the second division of the calendering factory was a Mr. Sirounian, a repatriate from Egypt with whom I had become acquainted. Through him, I was able to obtain a job there.

In February 1953, Stalin ordered that a list be prepared of all repatriates in Armenia. He sent a special delegation from Moscow to Yerevan to carry out the order. They began to visit all the homes and record the names. Stalin's obvious objective was to keep Armenia below one million and annex it to Georgia.

When members of the delegation came to our home, I was not there. Beatrice noticed that they recorded the names of the three repatriate families from America, but not the family of Simon Mekenian, native to Leninakan. Beatrice asked why. Those doing the recording answered, "We have been directed to record only repatriates."

When I returned home and got the bad news, I said to Beatrice, "Quick, pack the warmest clothes we still have into two suitcases." We were guessing that before long we repatriates would be thrust into the black auto and exiled to Siberia, as was done in 1949.

In a two-week period, one hundred twenty-five thousand old and new repatriates were recorded. We waited on the alert every night for what we feared would happen to us.

It was during this frightful period that our son Paul came from America to Iran in connection with his work. He wanted very much to travel to Yerevan and visit us for a few days. But the American ambassador in Teheran cautioned him: "If you go there, you may not be allowed to return, at least as long as Stalin is alive." Indeed it was dangerous to visit Armenia at that time. The doors of Armenia were closed to our own son and to any others who wanted to visit for whatever reason. They were days of dread and fear!

—Stalin's Death—

On March 5, 1953, I went to Yerevan's covered market to buy some food items. When I returned home, I found our kitchen full of smoke and soot. Alarmed, I asked Beatrice what had happened. She opened her eyes wide and said in a happy voice, "I am cremating Stalin." Cremating Stalin! I couldn't imagine what was in her mind. But quickly I found out why she was so pleased, even triumphant. We had a large Philco radio. She had heard a broadcast from Moscow that Stalin had died. Immediately she had taken a large picture we had of that dreaded dictator, broken it into bits, and stuffed the pieces into our coal stove.

Other housewives of Armenia did just what Beatrice did when they got word of the death of the monster (Stalin's own daughter's name for him). On holidays while he was alive, the Armenian people were required to hang his picture on the front of the house or on the balcony. Otherwise they would be regarded as anti-government and exiled to Siberia.

A few days later, I went to visit some Armenian friends

from America. They lived on a small street on the east side, just off Orzonikidze Boulevard. A large statue of Stalin ordinarily stood at the entrance to the Toumainian Elementary School there. Five days a week the teachers and children would pass under the extended arm of the statue as they entered this school.

This day I was astonished to find the statue had disappeared! As I looked just beyond, I saw that the whole thing had been shattered, with the bits strewn along the road. I soon learned that an Armenian tractor operator had put a chain around the neck and toppled the statue, feeling he had avenged the hundreds of thousands of Armenian victims of that monster.

Not long after, I had a similar experience when I was returning home by tram from downtown.

Standing on the highest hill in Yerevan, in the Recreations Garden, had been an enormous statue of Stalin, made of cast metal and mounted on a tall pedestal. The cost of constructing it had run into tens of millions of rubles. The monument, as it was called, stood dominant over the capital city, even over the plains of Ararat.

From the tram window, I saw that the monument was missing. Normally, it could be seen from virtually everywhere. Surprised, I turned to those seated near me and asked about it. A young man answered, "Last night, under the supervision of the commander of the Soviet military forces, two hundred Russian soldiers took the statue down. During the operations, two Russian soldiers died accidentally."

On hearing this, passengers in the tram made the sign of the cross, happy to be rid of the statue, thanks to Khrushchev. The Armenian people had faith that such events were a sort of miracle taking place, that in time

Armenians would gain their freedom, that an historical reawakening was about to begin.

Khrushchev had gone beyond just having the monument taken down. He had called on Armenian General H. Baghramian to go to Armenia with a troop of soldiers and remove all the Stalin statues. But the far-sighted general pointed out that Armenia was a neighbor to Georgia. The Georgian people were fanatically patriotic to Stalin. Many Armenians lived in Georgia. If an Armenian general carried out the mission of taking down all the statues, the Georgian people would develop a strong enmity toward Armenians. Hence it would be better for a Russian commander to handle the assignment.

Khrushchev, convinced of that wisdom, did place a Russian commander in charge of two hundred Russian soldiers who came to Armenia to rid the nation of all traces of Stalin's statues.

Beatrice and I, Yerevan, Armenia, 1953.

The two of us, Yerevan, Armenia, 1956.

162

The apartment building we built at 84 Baghramian Boulevard, Yerevan. This picture was taken in 1956.

The two of us in our apartment in 1956.

163

–XII–

A Welcome New Era

I was a day to remember!

Khrushchev and Anastas Mikoyan announced over the radio that Armenians had committed no wrongs to deserve being exiled to Siberia under Stalin. "It was Stalin who was guilty," they declared. Khrushchev said further that Armenians who were still alive in Siberia could return to Armenia at government expense and would be given free residences. Khrushchev rendered a great service to the Armenian people in making this pronouncement and declaring Stalin's guilt.

The Council of Ministers of Soviet Armenia was encouraged by what was happening. Orders were issued saying that henceforth if anyone accused another of slander against the government, he must have it confirmed by two or three witnesses. If guilt were established, the guilty person would be sentenced to five to ten years imprisonment. No Armenian would be exiled to Siberia.

The Armenian people heaved a deep sigh of relief. Feeling liberated, they turned their attention to the development and progress of the nation. And, except in Georgia, all the peoples of the Soviet Union busied themselves with removing any additional traces of Stalin.

At the same time, rumors began going around about Stalin's death. It was being said that his personal physician, on the pretense of providing a rapid cure for the dictator's illness, had injected and applied poisons.

Stalin had one daughter and two sons. One son had died on the German front. The other had been in General Baghramian's troops and had survived. This latter son, on Stalin's death, had accused Berea of being responsible for it and wounded him with a revolver shot. Berea's assistants immediately captured the son and imprisoned him.

Molotov and other high-level officials, however, removed the son from prison and began an investigation of Berea himself. A Stalin order was found in a drawer of Berea's desk directing him to "wipe out" Anastas Mikoyan. Stalin already had had his own wife assassinated, as his legitimate daughter later would testify.

The Georgian Berea, Stalin's associate and advisor, was branded a notorious villain, along with being immoral. It was found that he had been the instigator in 1936 of killing Aghasi Khanjian, the first secretary of the Central Committee of the Armenian Communist Party, a true Armenian patriot. As things developed, events and circumstances prevented Berea from carrying out Stalin's order to kill Mikoyan.

Finally, after thorough investigations by the highest Soviet authorities, Berea was executed. Not long after, Khrushchev and Mikoyan made disclosures and pronouncements on radio to inform the people about Stalin's monstrous deeds.

—*An Impressive Event*—

When Archbishop Gevorg VI was elected Catholicos of All Armenians in 1945, the Supreme Ecclesiastical Council and the delegates assembled for the election were unanimous in deciding to undertake a complete restoration of the Cathedral of Holy Etchmiadzin, located a short distance from Yerevan and left for centuries to the ravages of time. In order to accomplish this, a call for financial help was issued to Armenians everywhere. Despite noble intentions, however, the work of renovation continuously was put off because of the climate of fear that prevailed under Stalin.

But with Stalin's death, the picture changed. Through the efforts of Catholicos Gevorg VI, the government of Armenia fearlessly assumed the cost of the cathedral's structural restoration. Sadly, though, death broke the thread of life of that productive catholicos. He closed his eyes for the last time without seeing the work completed. This happened on May 9, 1954. Work on the cathedral continued, and the revered catholicos long will be remembered for his leadership in making it possible.

Soon after, the Supreme Ecclesiastical Council sent out a call to Armenians throughout the world to select delegates to come to Holy Etchmiadzin at the end of September 1955 and elect a new catholicos. Rouben Shahinian and I, both of us repatriates from America, were chosen from the Diocese of Ararat region of Yerevan.

There were some 150 delegates all told, and the assembly ran from September 27 to October 7, 1955. One of the principal orders of business at the opening session was to recognize with deep thanks the government of Soviet

Armenia's undertaking of the renovation of the holy cathedral.

The second session was opened by His Excellency Archbishop Vahan who announced that the agenda called for the election of the new Catholicos of All Armenians. He stated that under the canons of the Armenian Apostolic Church all bishops were eligible for election.

In the afternoon the delegates were led in procession to the cathedral where the election was to be conducted. Archbishop Mampre Sirounian read an oath repeated by the standing delegates. Then voting cards were distributed. These were stamped with the seal of the Supreme Ecclesiastical Council. One by one, we delegates approached the ballot box and inserted our marked cards. The box then was opened and Archbishop Sirounian read each ballot aloud.

By a wide margin—he received 125 votes—Bishop Vazken Baljian was elected. What a moving experience it was for each delegate to embrace the new catholicos-patriarch, wish him a long and productive life, and in unison sing the sharakan "Ech miadzin i Hore" (The Only-Begotten One Descended from the Father) while the bells of the cathedral pealed out the signal that he had been elected.

Immediately after the declaration of election, the new catholicos spoke. With deep emotion, he expressed gratitude for the confidence shown in him and offered this prayer:

"O, Lord, God of our father, show me how to carry out your will. Guide me in your path of justice. Help me in strengthening the Armenian Church and keeping it firm for the enlightenment and comfort to the souls of the

Armenian faithful and for the well-being of our fatherland. Glory to You for eternity. Amen."

The hallowed ceremony of consecrating His Holiness Vazken I as Supreme Patriarch and Catholicos of All Armenians took place on October 2. With crowds solidly packing the cathedral grounds, the colorful ceremony was a memorable occasion I shall always treasure as a participant and as an Armenian.

The remaining sessions were devoted to matters concerning the church, with major emphasis on preserving and building unity. A message from the new catholicos read:

"With warm feelings of patriarchal love, we call on our Church everywhere—the catholicate of the Great House of Cilicia, the patriarchates of Jerusalem and Constantinople, our diocesan primates, and all the servers in our churches and the faithful people—to remain true to the faith and traditions of our forbears, to remain faithful to love for the Church, to forever hold high the dedicated banner of unity among the people and the Church."

The final session was a reception for the new catholicos. It ended on a high level of enthusiasm and happiness.

—Need for Protection—

We had been hearing about stealing from repatriates who had come from America. A rumor circulated that Armenians from the United States were very rich and had brought a lot of gold with them.

Vahan and Vartouhi Mekenian lived in the first-floor west apartment of our residence building. When Vahan was away one day, a man came to their door. He claimed

169

to be a government inspector wanting to examine the Mekenians' passports. When Vartouhi was about to show the passports, the man drew out a dagger and demanded that she give him their gold. Vartouhi told him they had no gold. But the intruder didn't believe her and threatened her. In self-defense, she grabbed a knife from the kitchen table and cried out for help. The intruder wrested the knife from her, wounded her, and ran off. A week later, he was arrested and sentenced to fifteen years in prison.

Even from my childhood days, I have liked weapons. I always had had one, and many times had saved my life with it. The episode involving Mrs. Mekenian led me to decide I should have at least a hunting rifle. By law, citizens were forbidden to have revolvers, but on being registered as hunters, could own their own hunting rifles. So I bought a two-barreled Swedish hunting gun, although I had no intention of going hunting. It was purely for protection.

One day not long after that, I was home alone; Beatrice had gone to visit her sister. At about eight o'clock in the evening, there was a knock on the door. I opened it part way. Two men were there. I asked them what they wanted. They said my electrician friend Freddie had sent them to buy some clothes. Foolishly, I let them in, and they closed the door behind them. The Soukiasian apartment was just opposite ours, and the men led me to the farther side of the room so our neighbors couldn't hear what was going on. I told the men I had no clothes to sell. One of them said he was uncomfortable and needed to go to the bathroom. The bathroom was just opposite the door to our bedroom. I suddenly darted into the bedroom and closed the door. I grabbed my rifle, and quickly opened the door and shouted, "Hands up! I don't want to kill you inside my house, so get out!" The two fled.

When Beatrice returned, she insisted that I inform the police about what had happened. The police recorded in detail all I described about the two men. Two days later, the Mekenians' dog was killed. The following day, there again was a knock on our door. Beatrice opened it. Three men were there. "What do you want?" she asked. "We want to see father," they answered.

Quickly I got my rifle and rushed to the door. "If you are brave, come on in," I shouted. "I am very nervous, and my finger is on the trigger of my gun. Get out of here or I'll shoot you dead!"

As they ran, we could see that one of the men had a revolver in his hand. He and one of the others were the same intruders who had come before. This time they obviously had come to kill me.

After this second episode, I felt obliged to tell the secret police. Two detectives came and obtained full information. When they learned the details, they recognized who one of the robbers was. They had been looking for him in connection with another crime. I asked them to persuade the government to let me carry a revolver. They told me this was not possible, but they would see to it that we had protection.

The very next morning we noticed two men in civilian clothes patrolling the street in front of our residence. And when I would board a tram to go anywhere in the city, two unfamiliar men would board with me, one ahead of me, the other behind. They then would follow me constantly until I returned home.

A few days later, one of the secret policemen came to our house and enthusiastically informed us that word about the robbers had been provided to the more than seventy police stations around Yerevan and that surely the criminals would be apprehended. They emphasized that we did not have to worry; we were being guarded.

Three weeks after that, the same officer came to tell us that the criminals had been arrested and had confessed. They were sentenced to fifteen years imprisonment. On their release they would not be permitted in the capital city of Yerevan. They would have to live and work in a village forty kilometers distant. Also we were told that no dangerous persons would be permitted to pass by our house. "You will be protected 100 percent," we were assured.

In truth, seeing the care and concern the government was showing for our safety, our minds and hearts were put at ease. I expressed our deep thanks to the secret police for carrying out their promise.

—A Happy Reunion—

The closed doors of the Soviet Union were opened in 1956. The first tourists from America were coming, and among them would be our son Paul. He had written that he and a group of fourteen other persons would be arriving in Moscow on July 28. How wonderful it would be to see him after long years of not being able to do so.

In his work in the United States and abroad, Paul had found it difficult for persons associated with him and others with whom he was in contact to pronounce and spell the name Mugrditchian. Faced with the need for adopting an American name that would have some similarity to ours, he legally had become Paul Martin in 1954.

Although I was quite disturbed about it when I learned of the change, I realized that he had to do what was best for advancement of his business career.

Naturally, I wanted to meet the group at the Moscow airport. This meant getting ready in a hurry to leave by rail on July 23. Immediately before departing, it occurred to me that I should show Beatrice how to use my rifle just in case any need for it might arise while I was away. As we were practicing with it, I accidentally tripped the trigger and the bullet pierced my left thumb. The blood began to flow. We quickly bandaged it with a plastic strip; I couldn't let it make me miss my train.

As it was, I barely did get to the railroad station on time. And after a while, when the train stopped at Kirovakan for fifteen minutes to pick up passengers, I discovered in looking through my pockets that I did not have my passport. In the last-minute confusion of leaving, I obviously had neglected to pick it up from the table where I had placed it.

In shock, I decided to get off the train and return to Yerevan to get the passport. For in those days no one could travel very far without such a document.

Two young men were seated opposite me on the train. They noticed how distressed I was and asked me why. When I told them, they quickly assured me there was no need for me to get off the train and go back for the passport. They explained that they were officials in the Ministry of Internal Affairs and would take care of things for me when we reached Moscow. One of them had been an orphan in western Armenia. During the rest of the journey, I had many pleasant conversations with them. How fortunate and grateful I was for the interest they took in me and the help they extended to me.

When we reached Moscow, my two new friends took me to a small hotel and cleared the passport matter with the examining official. These two fine young men even took me around Moscow to visit important sites, including an Armenian exhibit. And they gave me their telephone number in order that I could call them if any problem arose for which I might need help.

Our son Paul had written that he and the other visitors would be staying at the Intourist Hotel. I went there to find out what time they would arrive at the airport and was surprised to learn they had come in the day before. A girl at the registration desk told me they were having dinner and directed me to the restaurant.

When I entered, I found the group seated along both sides of a long table. A woman across the table from Paul began looking at me intently as I approached him from the back. When I reached him, we joyously embraced, and she broke into tears. She recognized me from 1936 when, as a field worker for H.O.G., I had gone to Milwaukee and stayed at her house as a guest for three days. To think that we would meet again these many years later in far-away Moscow!

Happily, although it took some doing, I was able to join the group to travel to Tbilisi by air and from there to Yerevan by rail. This enabled me not only to spend wonderful time with Paul, but to help familiarize the whole group with the surrounding countryside and to tell them about Yerevan.

After the tourists were settled in the Intourist Hotel in Yerevan, I took Paul to our house. Many relatives and friends gathered there. We spent many happy hours together.

The group had been allowed only a five-day stay in

Yerevan. But through the intercession of the Vehapar catholicos, the ministry extended the time to ten days. In addition, the ministry assigned two men and an automobile especially for Paul and me to get around and visit interesting sites—Geghard, Sevan, Dilijan, and others. In Dilijan, we cooked and ate the ishkhan (famous "prince" fish of Lake Sevan), a special treat. What pleasant days they were!

Paul was an expert in aircraft maintenance and had become acquainted with the pilot on the flight from Moscow to Tbilisi. He was excited about suggestions Paul made for converting the aircraft so that it could carry twenty-four passengers instead of eighteen.

Indeed, Paul's aircraft expertise quickly became widely known in official government circles. So much so that a banquet was held in his honor at the home of one of the highest ranking officials in the Ministry of Internal Affairs. During the evening, Paul was asked many questions. I was so proud that he was able to respond to them in Armenian with very little need of help from me. Though he had been born and reared in America, he had not forgotten the language or his roots.

When the tourists left, Paul went to Iran in connection with his work. Although he knew things hadn't worked out for setting up the leather craft guild, we hadn't disclosed the details to him. We didn't want to dampen his spirits in any way. But we did give him our papers attesting to our American citizenship, thinking we one day might need them.

*Our travel guide and our son Paul, with me preparing
ishkhan fish from Lake Sevan, Armenia, in 1956.*

Paul and I cooking the fish.

—Finally a Break!—

During the days of Stalin, Beatrice had lost all hope of seeing her children and grandchildren. Her discouraged spirit had caused her blood pressure to rise to a dangerous level. With Paul's visit, however, she regained hope that one day she would see all of our family again. As a result, her physical condition improved. But unfortunately, the blood pressure situation had damaged the nerves in one of her eyes and she was losing sight in that eye. After many tests by different doctors, we were told that her condition was incurable.

Though it was difficult to face, the reality was that repatriating to Yerevan had not turned out well for us. Beatrice's health had declined. We had undergone years of frustration in establishing the leather craft guild. I had worked at different jobs to make ends meet. We surely had not achieved what we had set out with such high hopes to do in the homeland. Yet, we could not give up. I had to try again with the craft guild, this time with an appeal directly to Moscow.

In this final appeal, I set forth the good intentions with which we had come to Yerevan, explaining that our sincere purpose was to contribute to the progress of our Soviet Armenian fatherland by aiding its industrial development. I told how 153 written appeals had been ignored over a period of seven years, how uncooperative officials had been, how equipment in which we had invested had stood idle all this time.

When I finished the writing, I showed it to a government official with whom I was acquainted. He found it to be entirely appropriate, had it translated into Russian and gave me the names and addresses for six offices in

Moscow to which to send it, including Khrushchev and Mikoyan. Copies were mailed to all six.

A week later Industry Minister Kochounian's senior secretary, Mamigonian, rang our doorbell. I invited him in and said I hoped his visit was for a good purpose. It was indeed! "Minister Kochounian would like to see you tomorrow morning at ten o'clock," he said. "Please come to the government building."

There was no question about my accepting the invitation. I made sure to be there at the appointed hour. As I walked to the doorway of the building, Deputy Mamigonian was waiting for me. He greeted me warmly with "Baba jan, baba jan" (dear father). What a miracle this was! One who had been turned down for seven frustrating years in setting up a craft guild now had become "dear father!"

Mamigonian took my arm as he led me to Minister Kochounian's office. When we entered, Kochounian had me take a seat next to him. I looked at his desk. On it were two copies of the appeal I had sent to Moscow. One was the copy I boldly had sent to Khrushchev, and the other, the copy that had gone to Mikoyan. On the latter was a note saying, "Arrange Mugrditchian's guild matter right away. Make sure he is satisfied." The miracle was real!

With a reassuring smile on his face, Kochounian came right to the point. "Comrade Mugrditchian," he said, "you may make arrangements with the management of the calendering factory and sell your machinery and equipment to them. Also you can show them how to use the machinery." At long last a fulfilling break!

Two days later, the principal engineer of the factory, a man by the name of Souren, came to our house. With him was Mrs. Tamara, the assistant director. I agreed to sell for the value we had set, less ten thousand rubles as a gift on our part. In addition, I acceded to their request that I instruct them in the use of the machinery. Further, handicapped though she was with the loss of her sight in one eye, Beatrice began sewing fifteen different leather items as samples.

Every day over a period of a week I went to the factory to help them get started with production of the items. Initially, they sent the new products to Leningrad and Moscow for sale there. In six months, the factory had a profit of three million rubles from the items.

Mrs. Tamara visited us one day to express satisfaction and thanks for the assistance we had given them. I responded by saying, "Please tell the ministry about what we have done and the sacrifices we have made so that we can go on pensions. Our ages have reached that level." The government approved retirement pensions for us the following month, praising us for our sincere patriotism in serving the fatherland. I was given 560 rubles a month, Beatrice 445 rubles.

In 1959, on the grounds next to the government complex, there was an exhibit of products manufactured in Armenia. It included six items of leather goods we had introduced. These items were at the top of the show for three successive years.

Persistence finally had its reward!

–XIII–

Visitors and Travels

*R*elieved that things were going well with the leather items, we now could have a feeling of accomplishment in having come to Yerevan.

In this improved atmosphere, Hagop Mugrditchian visited us one day. He was a distant relative who lived in the village of Baghramian and had a family of four boys and three girls.

Hagop told us that his oldest son, Vartevar Mugrditchian, was completing required military service and soon would return home. He asked that we have the boy recorded in our household so that he could attend school in Yerevan and acquire a skill rather than become a laborer at the village collective farm. I gladly agreed to the proposal and said I would help with placing him in a suitable school.

Vartevar came directly to our house when he was discharged from the military service. I immediately looked into his interests and, according to his wish, placed him in a technical school. There he could study for three years, graduating as a specialist in electrical engineering. Through a friend, we also found a job for him, and I made sure he saved his earnings so he could have a family in the future. He lived with us as a member of the family. We took care of his every need as if he were our own son.

—Family Guests—

In 1959, our daughter Anna and her husband Vagharsh Bedoian, a high school teacher in America, wrote that they would visit us, with their two children, William (Billy), aged eleven, and Patricia (Patti), aged eight, arriving late in June. They planned to stay two months as tourists.

In those days, tourists paid thirty-five dollars a day at a hotel. It would be impossible for them to undergo the expense this would involve for the four of them over a two-month period. I wrote to them to come on their own as family visitors, rather than as tourists, and stay with us for the entire time.

In order to carry out this plan, I applied to the government in accordance with the law, pointing out that we had suitable facilities at our house and that we would take them at our own expense to visit important sites. After officials came to verify the suitability of our house, they approved the visit. As a result, the four did come, and what happy times we had!

My first step after their arrival was to go to the director of the local Intourist and apply for a car and driver. I told him I wanted our children to be well pleased with Armenia by seeing all the interesting and important sites and that I would pay all daily costs. He immediately agreed to the request and assigned us a car and an experienced driver named Ashot, who was from Karabagh.

Day after day, Ashot drove us to wherever we might choose. Each morning he would arrive at eight o'clock, looking forward to the day's trip. He was a fine man and satisfied our every need. He had a delightful way with our grandchildren.

All doors were open to us. We were free to go to places and take pictures. No obstacle was placed before us.

His Holiness Vazken I, Catholicos of All Armenians, received us three times. He and our son-in-law discussed a number of philosophical issues.

Anna and the two children enjoyed swimming in Lake Sevan. Vagharsh photographed them there. We ate the famous ishkhan fish in the Sevan Restaurant. The grandchildren especially relished the renowned fish. Vagharsh liked taking pictures of buildings. We visited Dilijan, the sanitarium at Arzni, important monasteries, museums, libraries, the famous monastery of Geghard carved out of mountain rock, Saint Masrop's tomb at Oshakan, the astronomical observatory at Biurakan, Dzaghkatsor, the zoo, the botanical gardens, and many other notable sites.

I bought Billy a tar and hired a tar instructor to teach him some music on days we stayed home. He quickly became able to play a few Armenian tunes, pleasing us with them. Also Beatrice taught him the Armenian "ayp, pen, kims" (ABCs), and these too he learned quickly. He could write a few names and easy words. In doing these things, he became imbued with the Armenian spirit. Later he became a subdeacon in the Armenian church and was graduated from Penn State University, where he earned a doctorate in anthropology.

Nearly every evening during the two months, our house was filled with relatives, visitors, and friends. It was a joyous time.

The walled-in garden in back of our house proved to be a festive place on days we didn't go on trips. There were abundant fruits to pick: grapes, apricots, plums, peaches, figs, sour cherries. Beatrice would put up these fruits in jars or dried in boxes for use during the winter. And our grandchildren loved to play in the garden. They would amuse themselves picking fruits and playing games. Billy liked to catch butterflies to take back to America.

—On to Moscow—

The last week in August arrived all too soon. It was necessary for our visitors to return to America, first going to Moscow. The parting was sad for us.

Because they wanted to do some sightseeing in Moscow, they would need an interpreter there. I suggested a young man by the name of Keshishian, who had graduated from secondary school with a gold medal and now was a student at the university in Yerevan. He was studying foreign languages at the university, among them English, Russian, and Turkish. Keshishian was a good friend of ours and came to visit us often.

Since our young friend could speak several languages, the head of the Yerevan secret police constantly was pressing him to leave the university and join the police organization. This placed him in an awkward situation and he didn't know how to extricate himself from it.

I suggested that he accompany our daughter and her family to Moscow and serve as their interpreter while they were there. When they left, he could contact the chief of the secret police in Moscow, explain his situation to him, and state that he had neither the desire nor the qualifications for the police work. If that high official would exercise the influence he had, the problem would be solved.

Keshishian happily agreed. I gave him five thousand rubles to cover all his costs. The key would be to get to see the chief, and I was sure this bright young man would find a way.

Many of our relatives and friends came to the Yerevan airport to say good-bye to our daughter, son-in-law, and their children. It was an emotional experience for Beatrice and me.

After three days of touring in Moscow, Keshishian went to the airport with our visitors and sent them off to America. Then he set about his mission of seeing the chief of the secret police.

He had no luck the first day. But our young friend was resourceful. He went back the next day and slipped one hundred rubles into the guard's hand. That changed matters. An interview with the chief followed. It was successful. The chief gave him a letter directing the Yerevan official not to bother the young man anymore.

On returning to Yerevan, even before going to his parents' home, Keshishian came to tell us what had happened and to thank me for my guidance. He had six hundred rubles left of the five thousand I had given him. We were much pleased with his success, and I made him a gift of the money to celebrate his freedom from the difficult situation that had distressed him so much.

He became a lecturer in English at the Foreign Language Institute in Yerevan, as well as assistant to the director of the university. He married and had two sons.

—Life Goes On—

Vartevar, who had been living with us since 1957 and whom I had placed in the School of Arts and Sciences, was to be graduated in 1960 as an electrical engineer. We decided we should be matchmakers and get him married to a nice girl. So we introduced him to Anahid, daughter of widowed Mrs. Azniv, a repatriate from Aleppo. Anahid had completed the ten-year school and had become expert in dressmaking. Vartevar was well pleased with her, and we arranged the engagement. But her former classmates were envious. Not long after the engagement was announced, they managed to steal the engagement gifts and other items from her mother's house.

Mrs. Azniv came to us and told us what had occurred. She was afraid that if the classmates came upon Anahid alone somewhere, something terrible might befall her.

To help overcome this danger, we brought the girl to our house and gave her my bedroom. I slept on the lounge in our living room (Vartebar had a room in the basement). This arrangement continued for three months. Then, in May, we held the marriage ceremony at our house in the presence of a large number of relatives and friends. The ceremony was performed by Komitas Kahana, and the best man was Abraham Abrahamian, who was one of my mother's brother's grandchildren. With loving care, the newlyweds and Beatrice and I lived together as one family. What a comfort it was to have them.

Not long after the wedding, my closest friend, Baghdasar Darakjian, came to see us one day and said he wanted to go for a summer vacation to the cities in Vladikavkas with their mineral springs. He had been there before and spoke favorably of bathing in the mineral waters. A relative living in one of the cities, Kislovodsk, had helped in arranging for the bathing.

In truth, I was in need of a rest. The idea of going there appealed to me, and Beatrice urged me to join my friend. A few days later, then, we took off by autobus.

—*A Memorable Vacation*—

It was absolutely marvelous traveling in the northern mountains of Armenia and part of Georgia. The scenes were magnificent along winding mountain roads and in lush green valleys replete with bubbling streams. Many important historical events had taken place in those regions. Of particular note, Russian armies passed through there to liberate Armenia and Georgia from the Persians and Turks.

When we reached Kislovodsk, we were put up in Baghdasar's relative's house. The mother of the family, a very intelligent woman, was a graduate of the American college in Kharput (Euphrates College). Her son was married to a modest Russian girl, and they had two sons. As children, the husband had taken both of the boys to Etchmiadzin to be baptized. One, still at home with them, was manager of a carpentry shop that built houses. He was an upstanding young man, and with his parents and the mother of the family, they formed a true Armenian household. The other son was a physician in the Ukraine.

After a few days, feeling we were crowding them, Baghdasar and I rented a room elsewhere. It had two beds and all the conveniences, proving most suitable for the two of us.

Kislavodsk, as well as the two cities nearby, Pitorisk and

We enjoy Sochi, Georgia, a Black Sea resort, August 1957.

*With my close friend Baghdasar Darakjian (on the right), in
the gardens near Kislavodsk, Georgia, in 1960.*

Zhlasnavod, was rich not only in hot mineral springs, but in pure, fresh mountain air. Nature there was bountiful and beautiful.

The famous mineral waters provided unique opportunities for cure and rest during the mild, sunny days of summer. Travel to and from the springs was by electric train, and very comfortable. The grounds were glorious, with gardens of colorful roses. Signs everywhere reminded visitors to "Keep the flower beds and the tree groves clean." Each day, the date, including month and year, was spelled out with variegated flowers arranged to form the letters and figures. People constantly were having their pictures taken standing in front of the display. We didn't pass up the opportunity to be photographed and have an unforgettable souvenir of our wonderful vacation.

All of the mineral baths had resident physicians. Each person had to undergo a physical examination before entering the baths. The physician at Kislavodsk did not permit me to bathe in them, much to my disappointment. He found that the blood vessels in my feet were swollen and said they might burst in the hot waters.

We went to Pitorisk, hoping the physician there would give me permission. But he also rejected me, giving me the same explanation about the swollen vessels. So we tried the third city, Zhlasnavod. The physician there was an Armenian woman, and we thought she might be more lenient. Again, however, I had the disappointment of being rejected.

Persistent, we went to the main clinic to have the Russian doctor in charge, also a woman, examine me. She checked me from head to toe. Victory at last! "You can enter the baths," she said. "Your heart is healthy and strong. But you may bathe in the hot waters for only five days, and from five to eight minutes a day. Then come back for reexamination."

How pleased Baghdasar and I were and how very much I enjoyed those five to eight minutes a day. And the reexamination brought more joy. The doctor told me I could bathe five more days, and from five to ten minutes a day. Suffice it to say, I not only was unharmed by the bathing, but it did me much good. The swelling in the blood vessels of my feet actually decreased.

During our vacation, I had opportunity to learn about the early and recent Armenian presence in the cities of that region. At one time, there had been quite a number of Armenians living in the area, and they had their own schools and churches. But, over time, they had dispersed. None of the schools or churches remained. Two episodes that occurred during our stay are interesting in this regard.

One day I went to a store to buy some apples. The clerk was a pretty black-eyed girl. After looking intently at her face, I said to her in Armenian, "Please measure out two kilos of good apples." The girl stared at me, dumbfounded. Then with a smile she asked how I knew she was Armenian. I answered, "Your beautiful black eyes and your lovely face, to say nothing of my internal electrical energy, told me that you are Armenian." We both laughed heartily. As we talked for a few minutes, she told me she was born in Karabagh.

Another time, as I was taking off my clothes to shower before entering the mineral baths, I noticed a young man in the next cabin. I looked at him, then began speaking to him in Armenian. He was astonished. "How did you know I am Armenian?" he asked. I replied, "My inner soul began to communicate with you, and in that way I knew you to be an Armenian son." Then I laughed. He turned out to be an Armenian from Tbilisi and was a goldsmith. We became friendly and took our baths at the same time. He told me much about the Georgians. His observation was that they were fanatically patriotic and worshipped Stalin.

The point is that everywhere one goes, there is a certain identity, an invisible link between Armenians.

—Home Again—

Back in Yerevan after a glorious vacation of almost a month and a half, I felt refreshed and content. But not content to be idle, by any means. There always were things to do.

The Black Sea was a place both Beatrice and I liked to visit. This had become possible after the deaths of Stalin and Berea, with our people given freedom to travel to the nearby republics.

One of our friends, Arshag Chakmakjian, had moved with his family to Sukhumi, one of the cities on the shore. Beatrice and his wife Lucy, with many common interests, were the closest of friends. Fortunately, they were able to continue to spend time together. Beatrice loved the sea air and would visit them during the summer months. I usually would join them for a week when it was time for Beatrice to return home.

One year we also went to Sochi, another of the shore cities, and spent part of the summer there. We rented a room and so much enjoyed the lovely sea breezes.

Whenever we visited such places, I was interested in gathering information about Armenians who had migrated there. And I always was curious about their present status.

It was evident that many Armenians, seeking refuge from the Turks, had gone to live in the cities and villages along the Black Sea. They had retained their provincial dialects. And after Stalin's death, they had opened eighteen elementary schools, with the Armenian government paying for teachers and textbooks. Students could go on to a higher education in Yerevan, again with costs underwritten by the government.

A happy event occurred in September 1961. Our Vartevar and Anahid were blessed with a baby boy. I was flattered that they gave him my name, Hovhannes. The baptism, performed by Komitas Kahana, took place in our home. Two years later, they had a daughter and demonstrated their devotion to Beatrice by naming the baby after her.

Thus we continued to live our lives in Yerevan, spending time with relatives and friends, doing some traveling, and observing with admiration the economic and cultural progress of our Armenian fatherland.

But, although our days were busy and satisfying, one extremely important thing was missing: the joy of being with our children. The visits of Paul in 1956 and Anna and her family in 1959 were such happy times for us. We yearned for more of those times.

–XIV–

Return to America

For several years, our children had been preparing papers that would enable us to return to the United States as American citizens. They wanted us to be near them, and that only could be possible if we were to come back.

They informed us about this in 1963. Beatrice, with tears of longing in her eyes, asked me to agree to the request. She said we had fulfilled our duties and responsibilities to our fatherland and had made many sacrifices in doing so. Also, she pointed out, we would be doing a favor to the fatherland if we were to let our pensions go to others. I agreed. I could not deny being aware that it was a time in our lives to be close to our loved ones.

It was necessary that we submit a request to the government to be allowed to leave. This we did. Our children wrote a personal request to Khrushchev.

A few months later, I was called to the visa office and informed that permission was being granted for us to return. Our visas were ready, but we were advised not to tell anyone about our planned departure until later.

It turned out that the assistant consul in the American embassy in Moscow had created a lot of difficulty in the

matter of getting our American visas. He had wanted doc-
umented proof of where and when we were born. This, of
course, was ridiculous! Our birthplaces were in Turkish
hands at the time. During the great massacre there the
Armenian presence had been wiped out, and we had left
those parts forty-two years ago. How could there possibly
be any birth records?

Fortunately, I had kept copies, complete with dates and
photographs, of official papers we had submitted to the
American consulate in getting permission to go to America
in 1921. These served a similar purpose forty-two years
later. For they were the basis of a strong letter I wrote to
the American embassy in Moscow. We had the added
good fortune of the assistant consul's having been replaced
by a Californian named Kirk. Soon we were informed by
letter that we were American citizens and could come to
Moscow within a specified time to leave for the United
States.

— *Preparations* —

We began getting ready for departure. Many wanted to
buy our apartment with its conveniences and large garden.
A new repatriate from Iran offered fifteen thousand rubles.
Another wanted the forty-gallon electric water heater and
offered two thousand rubles for it. An offer of eight hundred rubles came for the bathtub. All of these offers were
in new rubles worth about ten times the old ones.

It was unlawful, however, to take rubles out of the
Soviet Union. Each person could take only one hundred
dollars in exchange for rubles. Since this was the case,
Beatrice and I decided to leave our apartment to Vartevar

196

and his family. We already had repaid the loan we had received from the government, and the apartment was totally free and clear of any debt. So we proceeded with documents attesting to the gift, thus bequeathing to Vartevar, Anahid, and their two children the home we had built and loved.

Late one afternoon when we were packing to leave, Anahid began having birthing pains. Vartevar was still at work. Beatrice immediately took Anahid to the hospital by taxi, asking me to take care of little two-year-old Hovhannes. He was a smart child. In the mornings, awakening before me, be would run to our bedroom and place my slippers at the side of the bed. Then he would awaken me and lie down in my arms as though he had missed me. This was a ritual we both were going to miss.

As instructed, I took him to their bedroom and put him to bed at the proper time. To watch over him, I sat at the door near their room and waited for Vartevar to return from work. But I had left the front door open, and a draft was blowing through. Without fully realizing it, I became quite chilled. This led to a bad cold that got so severe we called Dr. Nargizian.

Dr. Nargizian had repatriated with his parents from Damascus and had continued his studies at the Faculty of Medicine in Yerevan, graduating with high honors. A most competent man, he was a specialist in internal medicine and heart ailments. After examining me carefully, he concluded that I had a bad case of pneumonia. He began to treat me with penicillin injections. And since they would be required every three hours, day and night, he taught Vartevar how to give them to me at night.

The doctor visited me every day. This was the fourth time I had had pneumonia. Besides the discomfort of the

sickness itself, I was being troubled by the frequent inser-
tion of the hypodermic needle. So much so after ten days
I asked the doctor to stop the injections if possible. He
examined me, said my lungs were not yet clear, and insisted that I have three more days of injections. I was so
thankful to be told after those three days that I was fully
cured and that my heart was strong. Dr. Nargizian advised
me, however, to be extremely careful about contracting
the sickness again.

Meanwhile, because of the delay caused by my illness,
the time limit for the exit visas given us by the Soviet
Union was nearing an end. If we didn't hurry, we would
lose the authority to leave for America and would have to
start all over to obtain visas. I didn't feel much like rushing. The effects from the penicillin shots still bothered me;
my head was constantly dizzy. There were many suggestions that we delay our trip. But with our preparations
having gone as far as they had, we elected to proceed. So
hurry we did.

—The Journey Back—

The date was November 10, 1963. The airport at Yerevan
was crowded with relatives and friends who had come to
give us a final farewell and send-off. There was much
emotion, knowing there was little likelihood of seeing one
another again. Vartevar had obtained a release from his
work in order that he might accompany us to Moscow and
be of help in the formalities we would have to go through.
He knew Russian well.

On arriving in Moscow, we took two rooms in a hotel,
one for Vartevar, the other for us. The next day, being an

American holiday, the American embassy was closed. So we went there the following day. Mr. Kirk, the new consul, received us and looked over our official papers. He told us our son Paul had sent us airline tickets and that they were ready.

"Let the American dollars remain in America," I said. "We have rubles to pay for the tickets." Mr. Kirk complimented us on being good Americans. I asked him where we could buy the tickets. He gave me the information, also the address of the Soviet Union office where we could go to confirm our exit visas and our American passports. Further, he gave us directions to a bank where we could change our remaining rubles to get our permitted one hundred dollars per person.

We went to buy the airline tickets with rubles, but the clerk refused to sell them to us, saying we must use the tickets Paul had sent us from America. I appealed to an official higher than the clerk. After much effort and argument, I finally succeeded in buying the tickets.

With all the formalities, we had to spend several days in Moscow getting clearance to leave. I was still partly sick and fully tired of going through all the red tape, but there was no choice.

At long last, on November 20, we were able to go to the airport to board a Soviet airliner bound for Copenhagen. From there we would fly the North Pole route directly to Los Angeles.

At the airport, customs officials began a minute inspection of our luggage and packages. I was worried about missing our flight. If we were delayed for long, that surely would happen. In my anxiety, I became vexed. Facing the inspectors, I said in an angry voice, "I have worked without recompense for forty years for the benefit of the Soviet Union, both in America and Soviet Armenia. And you have my detailed biography. Yet you are suspicious of our lawfulness and sincerity. I don't want to miss this flight!"

An elderly examiner looking inside our suitcases blushed deeply and closed them. He quickly ordered workers to hand over the luggage to the airline for loading. He did not examine my pockets. Before boarding the airplane, I took from one of my pockets five hundred rubles that I still had and some kopeks. I put the money in Vartevar's hands and asked him to give one hundred rubles to Beatrice's sister. The remainder was to be used by his family for whatever they wished. We embraced, thanked him for all he had done, and rushed to the airplane. The examiners were astonished by our honesty.

We took our places in the plane and landed in Copenhagen three hours later. It was a long walk to reach the exit gate. One of the passengers voluntarily helped us with our hand luggage by carrying my bag. He was a Dane and knew a little English. We thanked him for his thoughtfulness and help, and he was indeed a help because I tired easily from the recent illness.

The agent at the exit looked at our American passports and our airline tickets. He told us we were late for the flight for Los Angeles. We would have to wait until the next day for the direct flight. We were taken to the Royal Hotel where we were given a room and treated in the most courteous manner. Our dinner table was festive with two candles; it was a lovely last-night send-off for our return to America.

The next morning we were driven to the airport. The gracious treatment we received in Copenhagen exceeded anything we had seen anywhere else.

During the long flight, I had much time for reflecting on our years in Yerevan.

We had repatriated with such high hopes. Yet, what bitter disappointments and problems we faced from the very beginning, even in getting there after having made such extensive and costly preparations.

How unbelievably naive I had been in not thoroughly investigating what the actual situation was in Soviet Armenia—Stalin's fearsome and oppressive rule. The deprivations Armenians were suffering—the shortages of necessities, the unsanitary conditions, the black markets. The terrible housing in which we would have to live. The total indifference and obstacles we would encounter in trying to establish our leather craft guild, the utter frustrations we would have to endure, the dangers to our lives that would befall us.

There were so many negatives to regret. But in the final analysis, there were positives for which to be grateful: the changed, wholesome atmosphere that descended after Stalin's death and the invigorating meaning it held for the advancement of our little nation; our lovely house and garden and the festive times we had there with friends and relatives and visitors; the opportunities that had arisen to help others in the homeland and the good fortune we had in being able to do so; the seashore and other travels we enjoyed; and, at long last, realization of the goal we had in going there: success with our leather craft.

On balance, then, the good had outweighed the bad. We truthfully could say that Soviet Armenia and its people had benefited from our having been there. And that, after all, was why we had gone those many years ago.

We arrived in Los Angeles on November 22, at ten o'clock in the evening. Our children and grandchildren were at the airport waiting for us. Having heard that I was ill, our son Paul had brought a doctor with him. Thanks to the Lord, there was no need for the physician's care. We embraced all who had come to greet us. And soon we were on our way to our daughter Anna's house where we would stay as guests until we could get our plans in order.

The Mugrditchian Clan, November 1963.

Epilogue

All of us were happy to have our mother and father back in the United States. We wanted them to have many enjoyable years ahead being close to their loved ones.

They stayed for a while with my sister Anna and her family in Sherman Oaks, a suburb of Los Angeles. Then they rented a pleasant apartment there, soon making new friends. They also had become members of St. Peter Armenian Church in nearby Van Nuys, and Mother was asked to teach Armenian to the children of the parish's Armenian school. She thoroughly liked doing this, not only teaching them the native language, but fascinating them with stories of her childhood experiences in her Cilician homeland. She did this work until her failing eyesight made it impossible for her to continue.

Dad gradually regained strength and recovered completely from his long, serious bout with pneumonia. As new friends learned about his and Mother's lives in the two homelands, they urged him to write his memoirs. We family members joined in this urging, for we thought it would be wonderful for us, for our children, and for their children to have a record of our parents' colorful past.

Fortunately, he agreed to undertake the assignment. He had made no notes along the way, so it was a case of depending on his remarkable memory to recall the dates, incidents, events, and experiences he recorded with great diligence, a task that occupied him until his death in 1974.

We are grateful to him for this legacy, and for the comfort he and Mother brought us in spending their remaining years close to us. Mother went into a retirement home in Van Nuys after Dad died. In the mid-1980s, she moved to Florida to be with my wife Barbara and me. She passed away in 1989.

The title that has been given these memoirs—*To Armenians with Love*—captures the true feeling of the author throughout his entire life. In him was a spirit of patriotism that was steadfast to the very day he left us.

—Paul (Mugrditchian) Martin